LEARNING RESOURCES CI
VANCE-GRANVILLE COMMUNIT.   Y0-BAZ-846
P. O. BOX 917
HENDERSON, NC 27536

VGM Opportunities Series

OPPORTUNITIES IN **COMPUTER CAREERS**

Julie Kling Burns

Foreword by
George R. Eggert, CSP
Executive Director
Institute for Certification
  of Computer Professionals

VGM Career Books

Chicago   New York   San Francisco   Lisbon   London   Madrid   Mexico City
Milan   New Delhi   San Juan   Seoul   Singapore   Sydney   Toronto

Library of Congress Cataloging-in-Publication Data

Burns, Julie Kling.
    Opportunities in computer careers / Julie Kling Burns.
      p. cm. — (VGM opportunities series)
    ISBN 0-658-01638-5 (hardcover) — ISBN 0-658-01639-3 (paperback)
    1. Electronic data processing—Vocational guidance. 2. Computer science—Vocational guidance. I. Title. II. Series.

QA76.25 .B85 2001
004'.023—dc21

2001026427

VGM Career Books

A Division of *The McGraw·Hill Companies*

Copyright © 2002 by The McGraw-Hill Companies. All rights reserved. Printed in the United States of America. Except as permitted under the United States Copyright Act of 1976, no part of this publication may be reproduced or distributed in any form or by any means, or stored in a database or retrieval system, without the prior written permission of the publisher.

Portions of this book were previously published in *Opportunities in CAD/CAM Careers* and *Opportunities in Computer Systems Careers (Software)*.

1 2 3 4 5 6 7 8 9 0 LBM/LBM 0 9 8 7 6 5 4 3 2 1

ISBN 0-658-01638-5 (hardcover)
     0-658-01639-3 (paperback)

This book was set in Times by Publication Services, Inc.
Printed and bound by Lake Book Manufacturing

Cover photograph copyright © PhotoDisc

McGraw-Hill books are available at special quantity discounts to use as premiums and sales promotions, or for use in corporate training programs. For more information, please write to the Director of Special Sales, Professional Publishing, McGraw-Hill, Two Penn Plaza, New York, NY 10121-2298. Or contact your local bookstore.

This book is printed on acid-free paper.

CONTENTS

About the Author............................ vii

Foreword.................................. ix

Preface xi

Introduction............................. xiii
   Terms you should know.

1. Opportunities Abound 1
   Employers. Where the jobs are.

2. Careers Inside the Computer Industry 7
   Hardware product development. Software product development. Developing shrink-wrap and commercial software. Research and development (R&D). Working for a start-up. Marketing and sales.

3. Careers Outside the Computer Industry 29
   Employers and environments. Corporate software development. Systems analysis. EDP auditor. Operations. Information systems departments. System integrators, VARs, and consultants. Going independent.

4. Special Opportunities in Computer-Related Fields 47
Documentation: technical writers. Education. Medicine. Information science. Operations research.

5. Preparing for a Career in Computers 55
Preparing for the future. Learning on your own. High school. Two-year junior and community colleges. Four-year colleges and universities. Graduate study. Certification. Company-sponsored education and training. Keeping up with new developments.

6. Finding a Job in Computers................. 73
Researching employers. On-campus recruitment. Responding to ads. Using professional recruiters. Technical job fairs. On-line job resources. Resumes. Preparing for a job interview. Some practical suggestions. Evaluating employment offers. Intangible job satisfactions.

7. Shaping Your Career 87
Geographical distribution. Demand. Trends that may affect demand. Salary statistics. Advancing on the job. Technology and market trends.

8. Computer-Aided Design (CAD) and Computer-Aided Manufacturing (CAM)..... 101
Five major technologies. The CAD/CAM/CAE industry. How CAD works. What the CAD operator does. 2-D and 3-D CAD. How CAD and CAM fit together.

9. **Working in CAD** **111**
   The CAD field. CAD in industrial engineering.
   CAD in point-of-purchase.

10. **Working in CAM** **117**
    What CAM is. Workcell control software.
    Process control job opportunities. Expectations
    of graduates entering the field.

11. **Working in Robotics** **121**
    Growth in the robotics industry. Why robots?
    Service robots.

12. **Education and Training Lead to
    Jobs in CAD/CAM** **125**
    Job-hunting tips. Competencies and skills to
    succeed. Trends. Researching educational
    opportunities. Apprenticeships.

13. **International Job Opportunities.** **133**
    Software.

Appendix: Associations **137**

ABOUT THE AUTHOR

Julie Kling Burns is an independent consultant providing market research and analysis to hardware and software vendors, including Apple, Borland, Component Integration Labs (CI Labs), Taligent, and others. Her clients benefit from her twenty years of industry experience in developing and marketing software products.

Prior to launching her consulting practice, Julie served as vice president of marketing for PeerLogic, Inc., a communications middleware vendor. In this role, she established the overall marketing direction for the company, including product positioning, marketing strategy, and channel development.

From 1986 to 1991, Julie held a wide range of positions in product, developer, technical, and channel marketing at Lotus Development Corporation. She was instrumental in launching such breakthrough products as Lotus Agenda, the first PIM, and Lotus Express, a pioneering PC-based electronic mail application. As marketing manager for networked products, Julie developed a keen understanding of today's networked computing environment. She also spearheaded development of a reseller program for Lotus Notes and other networked products.

Before joining Lotus, Julie worked on office automation and data communications products for Data General and as an independent consultant. She was a tenured member of the graduate faculty at Texas A&M University and also taught business communications at California State University, Long Beach. She has been a featured speaker at industry conferences and seminars.

Julie holds a B.A. from the University of California, Santa Cruz, and an M.A. and Ph.D. from the State University of New York at Buffalo.

FOREWORD

The opportunities are endless for a person who considers a career in the exciting world of computers. Challenging and rewarding positions are available in every area of business and in every corner of the world.

The twenty-first century has opened doors for students in some industries that are relatively new to computerized techniques. Other doors will continue to open in established computerized businesses that need knowledgeable practitioners of the newest technologies. Imagine working on a cruise ship in the Caribbean or being part of a research team at IBM. These opportunities and others just as varied are available to computer science graduates.

The knowledge you have gained in high school is a substantial base for additional higher level education in computer science. By building on your knowledge, you can open many more doors in the growing and changing information processing industry.

Your career choice deserves all of the advantages it can use. In this fast paced, competitive business, any assistance you can give your resume will help move you along your career path.

Joining a professional society is one way to assist you in defining your career goals and educational development. Professional societies with student chapters allow students to interact with professionals who have been successful in this ever-changing field. By joining a student chapter of a society, you can gain valuable knowledge from seasoned pros, you can learn about the day-to-day operations in the industry, and you can pinpoint the specialized area of the industry in which you would like to practice.

Choosing a career can be confusing and a little bit scary. Julie Kling Burns explores the challenging and interesting field of computer science. Take advantage of all the information in this book, and then you will be able to offer only your best to one of the most exciting careers available today!

George R. Eggert, CSP
Executive Director
Institute for Certification
  of Computer Professionals

PREFACE

For most of us, when we think of computers, the image that immediately comes to mind is that of the gray or tan or sometimes tangerine, aqua, or lime-green case that sits atop our work desks or in our school labs. Computers, however, do come in a variety of sizes from the large mainframe computer, which can fill a room, to a microprocessor, which can fit through the eye of a needle. Large computer systems are valuable for processing huge amounts of data, such as engineering, governmental, or scientific data. And microprocessors are ubiquitous, found in virtually every electronic device imaginable, such as automobiles, wristwatches, telephones, video recorders, and much, much more.

Again though, for most of us, the desktop computer is the most common and versatile device available. With it we can do word processing, store and update a variety of data, play games, and keep track of inventories, employees, and customers. We can also use computer-aided design programs to simulate, say, how a new car design will handle wind resistance or how various medical devices can help alleviate physical disorders. These small but ever more powerful machines are playing a larger and larger part in our everyday work lives. Name your area of interest, and it is likely that a computer and a specific type of software will in some way be involved.

For those of you interested in desktop computing, we hope that you will find enough information here to get started on the career you have chosen. The first part of the book provides specific information on careers inside the computer industry, from developing hardware systems to working in research and development to striking out as an independent. You will also find out about computer-related careers in areas such as technical writing, education, medicine, and more. Finally, you'll learn about the education and preparation you'll need and the salaries you can expect to make in this burgeoning and important career.

The second part of the book zeros in on working in CAD, CAM, CAE, and robotics. The bent is definitely more technical, and if you have what it takes, you can use your skills in computer graphics to draw and/or design images that offer much more in terms of how a product will look and operate than any flat, paper-bound drawing.

As the first part of the book provided information on more mainstream computer jobs, the second part offers educational and professional strategies you'll need to succeed, given the more technical uses of computers today. Information on apprenticeships, opportunities abroad, and associations in this field will all combine to give you the edge you need in this fascinating field.

Whatever the area of computer expertise you choose, you'll find information in these pages that will give you an overview of what to expect and ideas to help you plan your career. We hope it proves to be an exciting and fulfilling one.

The Editors of VGM Career Books

INTRODUCTION

Computers are everywhere—in homes and schools, offices and banks, on farms, in supermarkets and airlines, in architectural and manufacturing firms—everywhere that people and ideas flourish. Artists use computers to produce graphics and special effects in movies. Computer games have a sophisticated computer in them. Computers help us in making plane reservations, phoning for business or pleasure, and can be programmed to write music or poetry. And that means that careers in computers can also be found everywhere.

You just have to know where to find them and which careers might appeal to you. For example, information systems professionals can combine their education in software and business analysis to develop applications that keep businesses up and running. Or you may turn your technical skills into sales and marketing or explore the opportunities in technical documentation, quality assurance, customer support, education, and even entertainment. Software professionals even work in publishing, television, and the movies.

Some careers demand a college degree; others require a master's degree; still others need a Ph.D. Some have found their careers in computers after attending a two-year college. The possibilities are almost endless because of the wide variety of careers available. You are limited only by your own dreams and talents.

Computer careers also are affected by the economy, especially the global economy. Downsizing in the 1990s and the so-called "tech wreck" of the early part of 2001 have left some startups and computer-related companies in the dust. But others will withstand the strain and endure, perhaps in another form or shape, but ready to bounce back and provide lucrative careers for those who want them.

All careers are dependent on a healthy economic environment, but since computers are comparatively new and subject to sudden and major changes in technology, anyone pursuing a career in computers should be especially aware that continuing education, networking, and memberships in professional organizations are particularly important in keeping up with the latest developments.

Although the computer takeover is relatively new, an older generation of computers, computer languages, and computer programmers still exist. Some more experienced programmers assert that younger workers are more in demand because they have real-life experience in using Java and XML as opposed to training courses as the older workers might have. The Information Technology Association of America reports that 843,000 IT jobs went unfilled in the past year, including 20 percent, or 168,000, in programming.

In addition, Congress recently passed a bill allowing twice as many foreign high-tech workers into the country who would probably demand lower salaries than older American workers.

More experienced workers may be more suited to project management, tech support, or programming with government agencies. Younger workers may be more suited to working on the developing technologies. Since this is a growing and somewhat volatile industry, anyone wanting to enter it should keep abreast of the latest developments in technology and the economy, maintain membership in professional organizations, and update skills as necessary.

TERMS YOU SHOULD KNOW

Computer science, like other fields, has its own specialized terminology. For example, *hardware* is the physical equipment of a system. Hardware specialists design and develop new systems, from chips to complete systems. You may have a background in electrical engineering or hardware design and work in the manufacturing sector of the computer industry. *Software* is the set of instructions (or *programs*) that control the system and tell it how to solve specific problems. Programs are of two types: *applications* and *systems*. Applications programs are sets of instructions written to perform a certain task or compute the answer to a particular problem. Systems programs direct, maintain, and otherwise assist the computer to operate and to execute applications programs. Windows is, for example, an operating system—an example of a systems program.

Most applications programs have been written in *high-level languages* such as COBOL, Fortran, or C. Today you can add Java, XML, and C++ to the mix. Computers understand only *machine language,* which means that high-level languages must be converted to machine language. *Databases,* or large organized collections of data, may store information for hospitals, department stores, or practically any subject for any company. *Networking* is linking computers to one another over wires to create a local- or wide-area network (LAN or WAN). *Multimedia* involves the delivery of pictures, video, and sound to a personal computer. Its content can be distributed on a CD-ROM or over the network. *Computer-aided design* (CAD) uses the computer to create, modify, or evaluate product design. *Computer-aided manufacturing* (CAM) uses the computer to plan, control, and operate the production of a product. *Computer-aided engineering* (CAE) helps engineers analyze and improve designs, through modeling and simulation, before products are actually produced. *Computer-integrated manufacturing* (CIM) uses a computer to coordinate activities from market forecasting, sales, and engineering through production and distribution. *Computer numerically controlled* (CNC) processes use machine tools or machines controlled by a computer. *Numerical control* (NC) controls processes automatically by interpreting data that have been prerecorded in symbolic form.

These are just a few basic terms that are necessary to understand certain concepts as you explore your opportunities. You will learn many more related to your choice of career as you increase your depth of knowledge of this industry.

The first part of this book addresses the computer industry in general. The second part concentrates on CAD/CAM and related technologies.

CHAPTER 1

OPPORTUNITIES ABOUND

As we now know, computer careers are almost limitless for programmers, systems analysts, operators, technicians, graphic artists, writers, and Web developers—to name just a few. Nonetheless, four major industries account for most computer-related employment:

- services
- manufacturing
- finance, insurance, and real estate
- wholesale and retail trade

However, computer personnel, in many capacities, can be found in transportation, communications, public utilities, government, and the military. And that's just the tip of the iceberg. As we said earlier, computers are everywhere, and increased opportunities for computer-related employment are the product of the expanded applications of computers to many fields.

EMPLOYERS

When you enter the career world of computers, you will probably work for either vendors (inside the computer industry) or end-users (outside the computer industry). Vendors include manufacturers of large and small general-purpose computers and peripheral devices or those who specialize in special-purpose systems and equipment. Within a vendor organization, these are some of the specialized functions:

- development
- quality assurance
- customer support
- sales and marketing
- documentation
- training
- end-user organizations

WHERE THE JOBS ARE

If you work outside the computer industry, you will work as part of the information systems team to provide computer support to the business operations of the organizations. Management information systems (MIS), information systems (IS), and information technology (IT) are terms to describe these jobs. For example, corporate IS jobs include:

- MIS and data processing
- the information center
- network administration
- data communications and telecommunications

Since companies of all sizes need IS professionals, applications experts can find opportunities in any corporation or business where there is a need for financial reports, analysis of business trends, or record keeping.

Anyone seeking a job in a computer-related field should go through these three steps in making a career decision:

1. Identify your skills, aptitudes, and interests.
2. Identify a career or profession where you can use your skills.
3. Identify the education and job experience you will need to attain your career goals.

While you are contemplating the possibilities, remember that computers are logical and they reward logical thought. If you are logical, systematic, and patient, and if you enjoy solving problems or puzzles, computing may be for you. Mathematical abilities can be helpful in systems programming, data communications, scientific and engineering applications, as well as in research and development. However, written and oral communication skills are very important in business and other applications. Positions in marketing, sales, customer support, or management also require excellent interpersonal skills. Some say that a more difficult but necessary characteristic to describe is a creative delight in making things work.

If you are still unsure about your place in the world of computers, see if you possess the following typical characteristics of a successful computer professional:

- a capacity for logical thought
- analytical skills

- mental ingenuity
- attention to detail
- persistence
- good communication skills
- creativity and intellectual curiosity

If you possess these attributes, together with a mechanical aptitude, and like the idea of working with computer hardware, you may want to consider the related field of electrical engineering. Or you may be more inclined to solve problems or want to learn about the theoretical problems behind a computer system. In that case, software may be for you.

If you like to work with other people, you may want to consider sales, marketing, education, or customer support. Or you might become a part of a project team that programs and tracks the flight of a space shuttle or develops special systems that enable blind people to "see" and the deaf to "hear" again. Then again, you might want to teach others how to use computers or help businesses to select, install, and maintain a computer system that meets their specific needs.

You also may be right for CAD, CAM, or CAE careers, separately or together, which offer job opportunities in an ever-increasing variety of fields. For example, nearly four thousand engineers worked with production personnel, supplier representatives, and airline workers in 238 design/build teams to create the Boeing 777. The most complex commercial plane ever built, this twin-engine jet could carry more passengers farther (more than six thousand miles) than any two-engine commercial jet previously had done.

The 777 was designed on a computer system that consisted of 8 IBM mainframes, 2,200 workstations, and a sophisticated design application that allows design engineers to create, configure, specify, and check parts at their workstations.

CAD technology also allows automobile manufacturers to see a concept for a point-of-purchase advertising display for a new-car showroom. Architectural firms use CAD and computers to shape a new and fundamental way that architects do their work.

CAD also is important to engineers to create 3-D geometrical models of lines and surfaces that represent objects in the real world, such as buildings or bridges. These models then can be precisely machined using CAM.

Surfing the Web shows many CAD/CAM jobs available, including design drafters, civil designers, structural engineers, CAD specialists, CAD technicians, architects, and structural engineers. Some of the many other career paths open to computer professionals include:

- artificial intelligence
- information technology
- software engineering
- computer theory
- operating systems and networks
- software applications
- programming methodology and languages
- computer graphics
- Web development
- database systems
- computer systems analysis

It is impossible to cover in detail each career, but we intend to give you a broad base of information to help you pursue your exploration of careers in computers.

CHAPTER 2

CAREERS INSIDE THE COMPUTER INDUSTRY

The kinds of opportunities available if you work for a manufacturer of computer hardware, software, or services include:

- hardware product development
- software product development
- research and development
- working for a start-up

In addition to these, we will look at a few of the many opportunities for people with technical skills to move into sales and marketing.

Because the computer industry changes so rapidly, it is impossible to cover every opportunity that exists. Rather, we will look at some typical career opportunities to give you an idea of what it would be like to work as part of the computer industry.

HARDWARE PRODUCT DEVELOPMENT

The word *hardware* is used to designate the physical units or equipment that make up a computer system: the computer itself and its network of microchips and circuitry, as well as peripheral equipment such as terminals, printers, and drives.

Computer scientists and software engineers work with electrical engineers and other equipment design specialists to design, develop, and test computer hardware and peripheral equipment. Design of hardware can range from the creation of a single computer chip, such as Intel's Pentium microprocessor, to an entire computer system or product. But since computers are made up of an array of microprocessors and memory chips, much of the work in hardware takes place at the chip level.

Peripheral equipment may be developed in conjunction with the computer design as part of a total system. Or it may be developed independently.

A hardware product begins as an idea or concept. A team of engineers and computer science experts get together and ask: "What would we (or our customers) like to see in a product? What problem can we solve?" Once the general idea is sketched out, a set of engineering specifications is developed. The next step is to build a prototype, or working model, which is tested, debugged, and perfected before full-scale manufacturing begins.

Once the performance specifications have been formalized, electrical and computer engineers develop logic and circuit designs. These patterns lay out the path electrons will travel as signals are pulsed through the chip.

Before chips go into full production, the prototype is rigorously tested to locate any potential error. Quality assurance engineers write special test programs to evaluate prototype performance.

Hardware engineers are involved in logic design and testing, microprogramming, systems design—linking individual chips into a fully operational system—and systems evaluation. All careers in hardware require a solid background in electrical engineering. You should plan your undergraduate program to include hardware design, electrical engineering, and physics courses if you want to work in this area. You should consider colleges and college curricula that specialize in computer engineering. More detailed information on careers in engineering can be found in VGM's book *Opportunities in Engineering Careers*.

SOFTWARE PRODUCT DEVELOPMENT

Recent breakthroughs in materials science and superconductivity, as well as continuing advances in chip technology, suggest that hardware development will continue to offer many rewarding career opportunities. Nonetheless, some industry experts think the astonishingly rapid advances in hardware technology may be over. They believe that, while hardware development will continue, the most exciting and creative advances in the future will take place in software.

Software Engineering

Development of feature-rich software will require a disciplined approach. This disciplined approach to the design and development of software is called *software engineering.*

Central to software engineering is the idea of the *software life cycle,* which breaks the design, development, and maintenance of large programs into a series of interrelated steps:

- identification of what the software must be able to do
- description of how the software will accomplish the tasks it must do
- implementation
- testing and validation
- operations and maintenance

The development of a new computer product includes following a product from its first idea through its manufacturing and marketing phases.

Software engineering describes both a method and a job classification. Many senior programmers working as part of a development team hold the title of software engineer. Software engineers usually have a degree in computer science (although this is not a requirement) and several years of experience designing software. Senior software engineers often are called architects, reflecting their role in determining how software will be built.

The Product Team

Programmers almost always work as part of a project or product team. This team usually includes a project leader or development manager, who may be a senior software engineer. The development manager often reports to a product manager, who is responsible for all aspects of the product, or to a department head. The project leader is responsible for overall program design and assigns programming tasks to other team members. This individual is assisted by an experienced senior programmer or architect who supervises other programmers, checks their work, and confers with the project leader when problems arise.

Programmers translate the design specifications into computer code. They work on small segments of the program at a time, writing the code, using sample data to test and debug each piece of code, and making changes to eliminate errors in their segments.

The most important goal of any project team is to get the product ready for customers and out the door. To ship a product requires the coordination of many people and many functions. Programmers must work in cooperation with other team members who help bring the product to market. Any product team will include quality assurance engineers, documentation staff, and marketing, in addition to development. It also may include a development or product manager. In some organizations, the product manager has profit-and-loss responsibility; his or her compensation may be directly tied to how well the product fares in the marketplace.

The quality assurance (QA) staff tests programmers' code and returns it to the programmer who wrote it for "bug fixes." Technical writers and editors work with programmers and marketing to produce printed and electronic documentation. The product marketing personnel work with customers to make sure the product meets their needs. They also work with advertising and public relations groups. An administrative assistant may handle the allocation of money, office space, personnel and equipment, as well as daily office routines. This frees the product manager to attend to technical design as well as handle business issues. A program librarian or manager may be assigned to keep track of the status of program modules and progress against the team schedule. A program manager also may work with manufacturing, distribution, creative services, and other groups to make sure everything related to the product is completed on time.

The size and composition of a product team will vary with the scope and complexity of the project and may depend on whether a company is organized according to function or by product team. Regardless of the makeup of the team, it is important for programmers to realize that many people with expertise in many different areas must work together to create a software product.

Most recent computer science graduates will begin as junior programmers or coders, working on a project that may already be well advanced.

Working as part of a product team can be an intense experience. Most projects are completed under extreme time pressure: It may not matter how elegantly you write a program. The point is to get the system up and running.

To work successfully under such stressful conditions requires more than mere technical competence. Patience, self-control, sensitivity to the feelings and concerns of other team members, and simple stamina are valuable traits in such circumstances. These traits may have little to do with a programmer's technical ability.

Systems Software Programming

Systems programmers specify, design, and develop operating systems, compilers, assemblers, debuggers, utility and database management programs, and other kinds of software that direct entire computer systems and enable higher-level applications to be processed. Systems programmers also install, debug, and maintain systems software once it is in place.

Employed by computer manufacturers, systems programmers work with design teams to develop new computer systems or products and to upgrade existing systems. They often assist in the installation of a system purchased by a customer and may help train the customer's employees in the use of their new system.

Working in an end-user environment, systems software programmers support their organization's computer operations and applications programming. They help applications people evaluate their computing needs and ensure that all systems function efficiently and accurately. They modify vendor software packages to meet the needs of their own company and sometimes are responsible for the security of the computer system.

The proliferation of personal computers and networking in a variety of industries and applications has created a need for systems programmers who can work with distributed systems. The systems programming requirements for a network of small computers differ from those of a centralized mainframe computer. At present, systems programmers with expertise in data communications, networking, database concepts, and client-server applications are very much in demand. Systems programmers work mainly with assembly languages or C rather than with the high-level languages used in applications programming.

People who go into systems programming tend to be more interested in problems in pure computer science than in the kinds of problems in science, business, or entertainment that are of principal concern to applications programmers. Systems programmers also need some interest in hardware.

Systems software programmers usually begin as coders working on programs designed and developed by systems groups. Then they may advance from the senior systems programmer level to systems project leader. Advancement in end-user organizations can lead to operations management and technical support positions.

Engineering and/or Scientific Applications Programming

Applications programmers working in a scientific or engineering environment design, code, test, and debug programs to solve specific technical or theoretical problems. These problems almost always involve complex mathematical calculations. Programmers in this field also help to develop the hardware, software, and input/output specifications for computer systems used in scientific and engineering applications.

Computer vendors employ engineering applications programmers to assist in product development and support. Some companies sponsor high-level research related to physics and mathematics. Engineering and scientific applications programmers also may work in many different industries, including aerospace and avionics, defense-related research and development, telecommunications, manufacturing, medical research and treatment, the oil and gas industry, and in all fields of engineering.

Applications programmers in a scientific or engineering environment may solve problems in "real-time" control systems, or they may write the software that links a network of computers and monitoring devices into a single, fully automated production line, or the software that processes the images beamed back to earth from space.

A programmer specializing in scientific and engineering applications should have a knowledge of Unix and will use languages such as FORTRAN (still used for scientific programming), C, and assembly languages. Ada, a language commissioned by the U.S. Department of Defense (DOD) to replace FORTRAN, also is used for aerospace, energy, and military research funded by the DOD.

In addition to a knowledge of assembly and high-level programming languages, you should have excellent mathematical skills to work in this field. You also need good interpersonal skills and the ability to listen. Scientific and engineering applications programmers work in tightly knit, small teams and often must confer with scientists or engineers to determine what their problems are, what input they can supply, and what output they expect. Because this kind of programming requires a high level of mathematical and technical knowledge, many people working in the field today hold degrees in mathematics, physics, or other sciences, or in an engineering discipline other than computer science.

DEVELOPING SHRINK-WRAP AND COMMERCIAL SOFTWARE

The bulk of software companies in the computer industry design and market shrink-wrap or commercial software. "Shrink-wrap" refers to personal computer applications that are typically sold to individuals through retail stores, direct mail, or other channels; shrink-wrap is the clear plastic covering that protects the box containing the media—either diskettes or CD ROM—and a user's manual. Of course, not all shrink-wrap software is distributed through retailers. It can come bundled with personal computers or customers may download it from the Internet.

Commercial software also includes products that are designed for large businesses and can be run on networked PCs, mid-range systems, or mainframes. Often, these products are developed for a specific "vertical" industry such as health care, insurance, or real estate. Or they may perform a specific business function such as payroll, accounting, or inventory control. More exotic kinds of commercial software include digital video and special effect graphics, as well as applications developed for the Internet.

Some of the most exciting and challenging opportunities in software can be found in shrink-wrap and commercial product development. This means that competition for jobs with these companies can be intense. You will need first-rate technical skills, the ability to work as part of a team, and a willingness to give up personal time in the interests of getting the product out the door.

Development Manager

Development managers coordinate all aspects of a specific hardware or software development project. These individuals plan, direct, and supervise the efforts of the project team. They schedule the work and write the progress reports. They also serve as a link between the project team and other divisions and departments.

Development managers need the technical background and experience that will enable them to assist in product development. In addition, successful development managers have exceptional interpersonal skills. This job requires working closely with a limited number of technical people and nontechnical support staff. It is up to the development manager to motivate employees, maintain group harmony and productivity, and build the team.

Promotion to development manager comes from senior programming and project leader positions. Development managers may have limited financial responsibility, but they are expected to remain in close contact with technical developments. The development manager position also can be a stepping-stone to the higher echelons of management.

Product Manager

The product manager has final responsibility for all aspects of a software or hardware product, including development and marketing. He or she has profit-and-loss responsibility and must manage the development budget, including revenue projections. In many companies, the product manager frequently has a background in marketing rather than technical management.

RESEARCH AND DEVELOPMENT (R&D)

Research is the study of the fundamental physical and theoretical problems in a field, without direct concern for practical applications. *Development* applies the findings of basic research to solve concrete problems or to design products that fulfill specific needs or perform particular tasks. Of course, the line between basic research and practical applications is never clear. In many vendor organizations, "R&D" is synonymous with product development. At the same time, however, advances in theoretical knowledge make it possible to develop new products. Furthermore, new innovations in technology may shed light on previously unexplained theoretical questions.

Most corporate research in computer science is closely tied to product development and manufacturing support. Much applied research takes place in vendor organizations, while the more theoretical research is typically done in university settings, often supported by funding from industry or government.

Positions in software research and development are available in nearly every area of computer science, including computational methods and numerical analysis (developing new algorithms and solving difficult problems in advanced mathematics); computer organization and architecture (devising ways to improve computer performance by changing the relation of a computer's parts and structure); systems design and systems science (studying computer operations and applications as a network of functions); telecommunications and network optimization; programming systems and languages (pushing the applications of computers in new directions through increased knowledge of programming techniques, linguistics, and natural languages); and information science (designing ways to make more information more readily available to users). Many positions in research and development require graduate study; some require a Ph.D. in computer science or a related discipline.

Current Directions in Research

The field of computer science changes rapidly. Today's topic of advanced research rapidly becomes tomorrow's product. As computer systems become more sophisticated, progress in one area of research often quickly leads to progress on another front.

Very large-scale integrated circuits (VLSI). For example, the microelectronics revolution that replaced slide rules with pocket calculators and placed the computer next to the television set in many American homes was made possible by integrated circuitry and the silicon chip. VLSI research covers work in basic physics, circuit design, materials and manufacturing, and in developing improved ways to link chips together. Breakthroughs in superconductivity research may have a far-ranging effect on chip design and manufacturing.

Neural networks and intelligent systems. Some of the most exciting and promising research today is in the area of cognitive science and computer systems, which seeks to understand how people learn. Neural network research tries to understand how computers can be taught to learn, in order to construct self modifying, intelligent systems. Work in this area combines psychology, neurobiology, and computer science.

Natural language processing and voice recognition. Computer scientists, working in tandem with linguists and psychologists, are trying to make it possible for people to speak directly to computers as they do to one another.

Image processing and pattern recognition. Many of the projected applications of advanced computer technology depend on teaching machines to "see"—that is, to recognize and identify shapes and objects and respond to that visual input.

Expert systems and knowledge engineering. Expert systems are software packages that incorporate facts about a subject and a human expert's ways of interpreting those facts. Researchers in expert systems distinguish between *data* and *information.* Data are raw facts: your body temperature, heart rate, and rate of respiration are data. Information gives meaning, significance, or value to raw facts. The knowledge that a body temperature of 104°F is dangerously high is information. Expert systems combine this information into a knowledge base and guide the processing of program input according to "rules of thumb" or *heuristics.* These rules of thumb are supplied by human experts and built into the software.

One exciting potential of expert systems research is that it provides a way for exceptional human knowledge and experience to be recorded, shared, and passed on to others.

Multimedia and hypermedia. Advances in computer graphics, compact disk storage, and other audiovisual systems have led to an interest in exploring the combination of sound and image reproduction with computers.

Human-computer interaction. An important area of research involves making it easier for people to interact with and use computers. Researchers in the field of human-computer interaction design the *user interface* of the computer system. Specialists in this field may work on the design of hardware or software. Mice, graphical windowing systems, the use of icons in place of text, voice input systems—all are the result of user interface research.

WORKING FOR A START-UP

A start-up is a small, new company developing a new product. The rewards for working at a successful start-up can be enormous. Many of the wealthiest people in the computer industry—not to mention the world!—earned most of their money in start-ups. The excitement of working on a new product, the greater control and responsibility one usually has in a start-up, and the more intimate working atmosphere of most start-ups can be almost as attractive as the potential monetary rewards.

A start-up also can be a disastrous venture for all concerned. For each start-up that succeeds, many more quietly fail, leaving their employees without jobs. Managers in a start-up are sometimes less experienced than managers in more established companies. Benefits may be thinner, and there may be less sensitivity in dealing with personnel issues. Still, the potential rewards for working in a start-up are enormous, and experience gained even at a failed start-up can prove useful throughout your career.

Employees in a start-up usually receive options to purchase stock in the company. Since the start-up's stock is normally not traded on a stock exchange, the options actually have no value until one of two events occur. Either the company "goes public," offering its shares to investors on a major stock exchange, or the company is purchased by another entity, which pays all shareholders for their stock. Neither of these is likely to occur until the start-up ships a successful product and begins making substantial profits.

Although start-ups usually have few true entry-level positions, their often thin financing leads them to value talented and energetic young engineers and programmers. If you are considering working for a start-up, you might want to ask these questions:

1. How much experience do the founders have in business? Have they ever run a successful business before?

2. How do the experience and skills of the technical leads stack up?

3. How is the company funded? That is, where does it get the money to pay your salary? If it is venture funded, how long can the company operate before it becomes profitable?

4. How comfortable are you with the risks of working for a start-up? How will you feel if the company fails or lays you off due to a lack of funds?

5. How much of your time and energy are you willing to commit to your job?

MARKETING AND SALES
Marketing

Marketing in the computer industry falls into three categories: product marketing, corporate marketing, and marketing sales support. Product marketing managers are concerned with marketing a specific product. They analyze the market potential for that product on the basis of the four classic marketing tools: product definition, pricing, distribution, and promotion. Product marketing managers determine how a product looks to the customer. They may be involved in manufacturing decisions, planning the product introduction, and working with advertising, creative departments, and public relations. Product marketing managers also will work with customers to guarantee that the product meets their needs, and with the sales force to help them sell the product.

Corporate marketing includes business planning, competitive analysis, forecasting of industry trends, and a variety of other tasks. In large companies, the corporate marketing group, managed by a vice president of marketing, may include marketing communications, advertising, market development, and vendor relations. Corporate marketing staff usually have business, rather than technical, degrees.

Marketing sales support includes a broad range of programs that help the field sales force sell, support, and maintain the company's products. This group often serves as a liaison between sales and product groups.

Sales Representatives

Sales representatives (or "sales reps") sell computer hardware, software, and systems. In addition, customers increasingly look to sales to provide support, training, and customization services.

To become a sales representative, you need a thorough understanding of computer hardware, software, systems, and applications. You must be able to judge the customer's needs to provide an appropriate system. Sometimes the customer organization will know its own computing requirements. Other times, however, the rep must start from scratch, working with a client who may know little about computers to define computing needs and select an acceptable product. Thus, the sales representative depends on his or her communications skills. Oral communication skills are particularly important, as the sales representative often makes informational and sales presentations and must talk easily with clients. In addition, the sales representative must be energetic, highly motivated, and willing to travel. Compensation for sales reps is generally tied to performance. A sales rep may receive a base salary, supplemented by bonuses based on his or her sales.

Sales representatives in the computer industry believe in their product and can back up their belief with technical knowledge. Most clients spend a considerable amount of money to purchase computing systems and are sometimes highly sophisticated computer users themselves. They expect sales representatives to spell out in detail all technical features of the products they are selling.

Education varies among sales representatives, though most jobs with larger vendors require a college degree. Some engineering-oriented vendors, especially those that sell to technically sophisticated users, prefer to hire people with a computer science or engineering degree, if they show sales potential.

In either case, a company's sales force will be exhaustively trained in the company's products. And training is an ongoing part of the sales representative's job, as new products are developed or present products modified.

Sales representatives generally move into marketing or sales management positions. District managers supervise the sales force and direct the sales operations for a particular geographical region or handle one or more special client accounts. District managers are promoted to regional managers. A degree in computer science combined with marketing and sales experience and an M.B.A. is virtually a certain ticket into executive positions.

Sales opportunities also exist with retail computer stores. Most of these positions do not require a college degree in computer science. Many may not require a college degree at all. Management of retail computer stores takes more specialized computer training combined with business education.

Technical Support Representatives

Technical support representatives provide a liaison between a vendor's sales force and the organization purchasing the vendor's system. Systems engineers focus on software problems, while field or customer engineers specialize in hardware. Before a sale, technical support personnel evaluate a customer's computing needs. They demonstrate equipment or software, help to write sales proposals, and generally assist the sales representative to deliver the system that best meets the client's specifications. After a sale, technical support representatives install the system and get it up and running and continue to serve as consultants to their clients. They may train users, resolve problems that arise in day-to-day use of the system, and function as troubleshooters.

Technical support representatives are salaried members of a vendor's technical staff. Unlike sales representatives, they may not work on a commission or quota basis. Clearly, though, these individuals play an important role in the sales function. Although the sales force may sell the system, the technical support representatives ensure that it does what it is supposed to do. The reputation of a vendor is often based on the adequacy of its field technical support.

Most vendors prefer to hire technical support representatives who have a four-year computer science or related technical degree, although some marketing personnel may move into this area if they develop enough skill in handling technical problems. Technical support representatives must be flexible enough to learn about the client's businesses in order to understand their computing needs. And because so much of a technical support representative's job involves talking with their customers and giving presentations, excellent oral communication skills are necessary, as well as the ability to adapt to the customer's environment.

Technical support representatives usually undergo extensive training in their company's hardware and/or software, and in other subjects important for developing workable systems, such as networking and telecommunications. These positions are a good choice for the individual who wishes to work with people as well as with systems.

Advancement opportunities from technical support can lead to either management or technical positions. From technical support, some people will move into sales and advance to manage marketing and technical support activities. Those who enjoy the technical challenges of this job will advance to advisory, senior, or consulting levels in systems and customer engineering.

CHAPTER 3

CAREERS OUTSIDE THE COMPUTER INDUSTRY

The greatest demand for computer employees comes from the business world. The most powerful and impressive effect the computer has on contemporary life is the degree to which it makes more information available, to more people and more quickly than ever before. The computer also provides tools that allow people to search, organize, and use information in entirely new ways. The computerization of the financial world, for instance, has profoundly affected the ways we access, spend, and invest our money. Automated funds transfer, automatic tellers, and up-to-the minute computer processing have changed the ways we interact with banks. The stock and bond market also has changed profoundly as a result of computerization.

The use of computers and information technology has changed the very structure of American corporations. Today, information is a company's most vital resource. The computerization of businesses has led to flatter management structures, organizations in which the management and analysis of information are critical to corporate survival.

In this chapter, we look at opportunities found in helping organizations develop and maintain their information systems.

EMPLOYERS AND ENVIRONMENTS

Most employers may be classified as either business, government, or nonprofit. The kind of employer you work for can have a profound effect on the course of your career.

Business

Business is the largest source of computer-related jobs. The atmosphere here is likely to be more competitive than in the other groups. There can be more risk and less security due to acquisitions, mergers, downsizing, and a changing competitive environment. At the same time, businesses often pay more than other kinds of employer. Raises and promotions in the business environment are usually based on performance, and opportunities for advancement may be more plentiful than in a government or nonprofit setting.

It is worth mentioning that both government and nonprofit institutions frequently turn to business for computer technology. By working for a government contractor, or for a computer-related business whose customers are nonprofits, you may be able to enjoy some of the intangible benefits of nonprofit or government work, while still earning a competitive salary.

Government

Promotions in government are based more on seniority and less on merit than in business. A government job may offer you the opportunity to use your computer science expertise on large and important projects, in areas such as social security, the military, air traffic control, and space travel. Government positions are usually more secure than jobs in the private sector because of civil service regulations.

Nonprofit Organizations

The nonprofit employment sector is vast. It includes most educational and health care institutions, as well as an infinite variety of advocacy, political, charitable, and religious organizations.

Working for a nonprofit can be much like working in business, but it also can offer nonmonetary rewards that are uncommon in the business world. In the educational environment, you might contribute to advanced research or gain satisfaction from teaching. In other nonprofit positions, you may experience the rewards of helping others. It is hazardous to generalize about such a diverse sector, but jobs that offer the greatest intangible rewards often will have a lower pay scale than similar positions in private industry.

CORPORATE SOFTWARE DEVELOPMENT

Corporate or "in-house" developers design, code, test, and debug the applications that help their company perform its business functions. They may help to design overall information processing systems and to organize the ways that information is handled and processed within an organization.

Many positions in business data processing are identified by the title programmer-analyst. This job title can mean different things in different companies. In small companies with small computers, programmer-analyst may be the main job category. This person will do routine programming. He or she also will design, maintain, and supervise all aspects of data processing operations.

In other situations, the title programmer-analyst represents the growing recognition on the part of businesses of the importance of systems analysis and systems integration—that is, getting the best software and making it work most effectively.

Finally, in large companies, the title programmer-analyst may be little more than an indication of status: a level of promotion above the entry-level category of programmer.

Successful corporate developers combine a knowledge of business applications tools with a background in accounting, finance, or other business-related subjects. If you are considering this field, you should take business courses in college and might want to consider a business minor. You also might want to consider a college major in information systems (IS) or systems sciences, rather than in computer science.

As a corporate developer, you need excellent interpersonal skills because you often will have to talk with people in many different departments of your company. You may have to instruct and supervise others, and you will certainly have to provide management with the succinct, easily understandable reports they expect.

As a corporate developer, you typically begin as a programmer-trainee or beginning programmer, if you work in a larger organization. You advance to chief or senior programmer, programmer-analyst, systems analyst, and into information management. It is not unusual for successful individuals to move into senior management positions. People begin as programmers; for the most part, they do not remain at this level. But for the right kind of individual, business applications programming is an excellent place to start. More opportunities are available in this field than to any other group of computer professionals. And openings exist in virtually every industry.

SYSTEMS ANALYSIS

Systems analysts solve problems and design systems to improve the efficient handling of information, people, materials, and machines in business and industrial settings. Systems analysts look at an area of a company's operations that is wasting time, causing trouble, or costing too much money. Employing various analytical techniques, including cost accounting, sampling, interviewing, and computerized model building, they define the problem, come up with a solution, and report their proposed improvements to management. They use their computer expertise to study and improve a department, process, or situation that they conceive of as a system, or interconnected series of conditions and events.

Systems analysts work in industrial and manufacturing environments as well as in business. In this sphere, a systems analyst is similar to an industrial engineer. For instance, a systems analyst may look at a factory and discover there is a problem in the flow of raw materials that is slowing down production. To solve this problem, the systems analyst would come up with a method to guarantee that enough materials are on hand to keep the plant operating at its most cost-effective level of productivity.

As you can see, systems analysts are generalists. They may find themselves working in a variety of areas within an organization. They might work in accounting and finance departments, or in administration, purchasing and inventory control, manufacturing and production, sales and marketing, even personnel management.

Systems analysts combine their knowledge of computer languages and systems with practical knowledge of the area in which they work. An ability to learn, a breadth of knowledge, and a store of practical experience are important keys to success in systems analysis.

The majority of systems analysts are employed by manufacturing and processing companies, banks, and financial or insurance organizations. Some work for consulting firms or system integrators. Systems analysts also work for public utility and transportation companies and for the federal government.

Preferably, systems analysts have an undergraduate degree in computer science or information systems. A few colleges offer undergraduate degrees in systems analysis. Some systems analysts have a degree in business supported by significant college course work in computer science. Many systems analysts complete a fifth year of study beyond their bachelor's degree in a business-related subject, and an M.B.A. can be an additional asset to a career in systems analysis.

Most systems analysts begin as programmers, advance to programmer-analysts, and are promoted to systems analysts after some time on the job. Senior and lead systems analysts work with clients and managements; they supervise other systems analysis staff as well as programmers and other information management personnel. They may advance to become manager of systems analysis, supervising all systems-related projects within an organization.

Advancement in systems analysis is based on an individual's ongoing education in the latest information technology and resource management techniques. In-house training, seminars and special courses offered by computer vendors and professional organizations, and reading professional publications help the systems analyst to stay informed about new developments. Success in systems analysis demands a high level of professional commitment.

EDP AUDITOR

EDP (electronic data processing) auditors are the watchdogs of large data processing systems. EDP auditors help their companies reduce financial losses attributable to data processing operations and guard against future losses.

EDP auditors locate irregularities, errors, and fraud in information processing systems. These errors may be something as innocent as a typing mistake or hardware malfunction. Errors of a graver nature are the EDP auditor's target as well. Unacceptable accounting methods, unauthorized access to computer files, or outright fraud are detected and reported to upper management.

About three-fourths of an EDP auditor's time is spent collecting information. The auditor interviews information processing personnel, administers questionnaires to system users, checks the computer programs to find errors or potential problems in coding, and verifies that all information on file is correct and up-to-date.

Clearly, an EDP auditor must be able to program well and must fully understand computer operations. He or she will have a broad background in business applications programming and will have worked on a variety of systems. In addition, a good EDP auditor must understand accounting and financial practices and keep up-to-date on the latest auditing techniques.

Communication and interpersonal skills are exceedingly important to an EDP auditor. He or she often must report unpleasant facts to upper management and has to be able to talk with programmers, accountants, and other information systems personnel about what they do without arousing their defensiveness or antagonism.

To become an EDP auditor, you need an undergraduate degree in computer science or in business with considerable computer course work. You also usually need at least two years' experience in the design, programming, and operations of large business systems. An M.B.A. degree or certification as a CPA (Certified Public Accountant) is an added qualification. Work in EDP auditing can lead to higher-level corporate management or to consulting.

Database Manager

The database specialist builds and maintains a large, cross-referenced library of computerized information using a special kind of software, called a *database management system* (DBMS). A database can integrate a number of separate files and records, making information instantaneously available to users.

The database specialist designs a software system to combine these records into a single, efficient data structure (or system of files), and makes sure that each department can quickly retrieve just the information it needs. In other words, the database specialist is a kind of resource police officer, managing information and making sure the database is both usable and useful for those who need it. In smaller organizations, the database manager (sometimes called a database administrator) may have no staff or budget. In larger operations, a database manager may supervise other database programming specialists and will work within a budget allocated for information management.

Database specialists get the essential information to the users who need it, and keep unauthorized users from retrieving confidential or classified data. In some installations, database specialists may be in charge of overall computer security.

Trends that support the need for database specialists include "data warehousing" and the increased use of executive information systems (EIS). Data warehouses are custom versions of the much larger version of a company's information, information that could be spread over many different sites. A data warehouse brings the data together for a specific use often by EIS software.

Database specialists work in large companies. They also are employed by companies providing information management services and in consulting. To become a database manager, you need several years of technical and business data processing experience and an expert knowledge of data structures, programming languages, and operating systems.

Director, Information Systems

The IS director is an executive who spends most of his or her time directing all aspects of information systems and processing within an organization. Advancing from systems and information management positions, the IS director hires and supervises systems and applications programmers, systems analysts, and other personnel. He or she assesses overall information processing needs and makes recommendations for system improvements. The IS director is principally responsible for budgeting for data processing staff and operations. He or she writes proposals and reports concerning improved systems operations and answers to high-level management.

Achievement of this position represents many years of management experience. In larger organizations, an individual is promoted to director of IS only after gaining considerable experience in systems management. The IS manager must know a good deal about the particular industry in which he or she works. Large organizations look for job candidates with technical and business skills, and tend to favor the candidate with an M.B.A.

OPERATIONS

The operations staff works in a computing or information center to keep the computer system running and applications software available. In a small facility, one college-trained individual may be responsible for every aspect of computer operations. In large computing centers, the staff can be sizable, with a resultant range in job titles and specializations.

Operators keep track of computer operations and networks. Operators coordinate the flow of jobs through the system. They mount and dismount the tapes or disks that store programs, input, and output, and make sure that all equipment is operating smoothly. When something goes wrong, operators attempt to restore normal operations or notify the person in charge of troubleshooting—usually the operations manager. Because operators know their system so well, their description of breakdowns can be essential in returning the system to working order.

Hardware technicians service and maintain the PCs, other computers, printers, modems, drives, and other equipment. Librarians catalog and file floppy disks and CDs, keep this material in good condition, and retrieve it as it is needed for specific jobs. Program librarians are responsible for cataloging and maintaining programs.

The technical support staff maintains systems software and deals with any problems that can be traced to that software, writes customized programs for special purposes, and works with end-users.

Today, operators, operations managers, and members of the technical support staff are all expected to have a high degree of technical knowledge and experience. This generally translates into a college degree in computer science or a computer-related subject.

Computing or Information Center Operations Management

The manager of a computing or information center directs and oversees all aspects of computer operations. The main responsibility is to keep the computer—peripheral equipment, data communications system, and software—in good working order.

The operations manager almost always works in mid- to large-sized organizations, and most operations managers work with mainframe and minicomputers in large-scale database and communications-oriented environments. The operations manager coordinates these diverse demands on the system and ensures that it functions for all purposes and all users In smaller installations, the operations manager's responsibilities are much the same, although the size of his or her staff and the range of system applications are more limited.

Although the operations manager is part supervisor, this job remains essentially technical in nature. To work with the machines, the operations manager must have a high level of hardware, operating systems software, and data communications expertise and a good deal of practical experience with large computer systems. This job also takes a certain amount of psychological resilience, for the operations manager must answer for any problem in the system. In the final analysis, when something goes wrong and the system goes down, it is the operations manager's problem.

Technical Support Services Management

The technical support staff is responsible for maintaining the operating systems software of an intermediate to large computer center. The manager of the technical support group supervises systems software programmers, schedules work, assists in troubleshooting, and takes part in planning and evaluating the overall system. If additional hardware or software is being considered, the technical support manager will be involved in the purchase decision. He or she also talks with users who are having problems running their applications programs on the system and with vendors of systems software packages to find out what might be causing a particular problem and how it can be fixed.

To become the manager of a technical support group, you need considerable experience in systems support. Commonly, the manager is promoted from within the support group staff. You must be willing to supervise and account for the work done by your staff and be acutely aware of the technical niceties and limitations of your system and its software. This position is not one for people who are easily frustrated, as discovering the reason for a glitch often takes all the skill and patience of a master detective, as well as an almost intuitive understanding of the system. For those problem-oriented, creative systems programmers who want to stay in primarily technical positions, technical support management is a good career goal.

INFORMATION SYSTEMS DEPARTMENTS

Programmers and programmer/analysts in most information systems departments are guided by project leaders. Groups of specialists in documentation, communications, and database management also may be directed by supervisors.

Since corporate development projects typically have a beginning and end, assembling project teams as they are needed has become a practical way for designing, coordinating, and testing new and revised systems.

The head of all of these information systems functions may be called the chief information officer, or CIO. This person must work closely with the top executives of all activities of the organization to see that their individual needs are well served by the information services department.

SYSTEM INTEGRATORS, VARS, AND CONSULTANTS

System integrators, VARs (value-added resellers), and consultants all offer services to large and small companies. System integrators (as the name suggests) focus on integrating the wide range of hardware, networking software, and applications that a company may use. System integrators also may resell equipment and software as part of their services. VARs provide many of the same services for their clients, although a larger portion of their income generally comes from sales and support, rather than from consulting services. Consultants primarily sell their time and knowledge, although some also may resell products. As you can see, these titles overlap to provide many of the same services.

Consulting organizations range from large traditional accounting and management consulting companies to small local firms with only a handful of employees. Some consultants offer a broad range of information systems practices; others focus on specific areas of expertise like risk management, network integration, or application development.

Working with clients requires well-developed interpersonal skills. You are often working at your client's site and serve as an ambassador for your company.

Working for a consulting firm, VAR, or integrator can have many advantages. The larger international consultancies offer a certain prestige, coupled with an opportunity to develop your technical skills in a highly charged environment. Working for smaller firms provides an opportunity to work at a variety of customer sites and on many different kinds of projects. In many cases, you will be able to see clearly the positive results of your work.

GOING INDEPENDENT

An increasing number of high-tech professionals work as independent or quasi-independent contractors. This trend is especially evident in software development and software testing. Contractors give up the security of a full-time job for the higher pay and greater flexibility of working on a hourly basis or by the project. They work for computer vendors, as well as for other businesses and in other industries.

Although contractors earn more per hour than most permanent employees, they receive none of the benefits usually associated with full-time employment. Contractors do not receive vacation pay, paid holidays, or paid sick leave. Contractors must arrange their own health insurance and retirement plans. Because the employer or client withholds no taxes from contractors' pay, contractors must calculate their own estimated taxes and pay them on a quarterly basis. Some companies spend considerable sums on continuing education for their employees, yet contractors must spend their own money to keep up-to-date.

Contractors also must look for a new job far more frequently than most people who work as permanent employees. A contract might last as little as a month or as long as a year; most are in the three- to six-month range. Between jobs, contractors have no income at all and may need to spend a great deal of time and effort searching and interviewing for a new contract.

Despite the disadvantages, contracting can be highly rewarding. Working on many projects for different companies contributes to the richness of a contractor's experience and provides a broader view of the industry. Contractors who work on an hourly basis are paid for all hours actually worked, unlike salaried employees who sometimes may feel exploited when they are asked to work long hours without additional compensation. And it can be satisfying to be in control of one's own business, however small it may be.

CHAPTER 4

SPECIAL OPPORTUNITIES IN COMPUTER-RELATED FIELDS

Here are a few of the exciting opportunities that may await you in computer-related fields.

DOCUMENTATION: TECHNICAL WRITERS

Technical writers combine a scientific or technical knowledge with an ability to write effectively. In the computer industry, technical writers provide *documentation,* the reference and users' manuals and other documents that support and explain computer products. Documentation helps the user, who may know little about computers, to understand and use hardware and software applications.

Many fields, including aerospace, manufacturing, and government, as well as all areas of engineering, need individuals who can communicate specialized information to many different types of readers. Because of the spectacular growth of computer use in the workplace and the home, writers of computer documentation are in considerable demand.

People who begin their careers as technical writers may advance into managerial or administrative positions directing a technical writing group or publications department and coordinating document production.

Employers are always eager to hire individuals with good communications skills. In a competitive job market, the applicant who can communicate effectively has a clear advantage. If you would like to combine your interest in computers with technical writing, you should take as many courses in journalism and English composition as you can. Courses in technical writing and editing and in publications production are especially recommended. Many colleges now offer graduate programs in technical writing; some even offer undergraduate specializations in this field.

The Society for Technical Communication (901 North Stuart Street, Suite 904, Arlington, VA 22203, www.stc.org) is a professional association that advances the arts and sciences of technical communications. This organization is a good source for additional information on this subject.

EDUCATION

Many opportunities in computer education exist within private industry and in public and private schools at all levels.

Vendors of computer hardware and software employ instructors to conduct in-house training and to teach those who purchase their products how to use them. For many vendors, customer training is central to their sales effort.

In-house company course instructors develop curricula and lead seminars and training sessions for employees and customers. These individuals often have advanced technical knowledge and the ability to share it with others. Customer training personnel combine their technical know-how with well-developed interpersonal skills. Oral communication and teaching abilities may be more important in customer training than advanced technical training. Thus these individuals may not hold college degrees in computer science. They may move into customer training from technical writing, technical support, marketing, or sales positions.

Depending on the company and its customers, training positions may require considerable travel. Certainly, to do well in customer training, you must enjoy helping others to master basic aspects of computer use.

Large companies often have an educational services department or division. In addition to coordinating all aspects of company training programs, this division may produce instructional materials, such as interactive tutorials on CD ROM, instruction guides, videocassettes, or films. Increasingly, companies are outsourcing training to other companies that specialize in technical education.

In public and private education, opportunities to teach students how to use computers exist at both elementary and secondary levels. And through computer-aided instruction (CAI), the computer can become a tool for teaching other subjects. CAI software has been written to teach everything from elementary arithmetic and spelling to advanced courses in fields as diverse as engineering fundamentals, foreign languages, and the anatomy of the brain.

At the college and university level, the shortage of qualified computer science professors is severe. College teaching is not always as financially rewarding as working in industry, but it does offer satisfactions of other sorts.

College instructors introduce students to the study of computers, encourage their interest, and help to educate them to become productive professionals. They teach students from a variety of majors to understand how computers work and how they influence society. In addition to their teaching, professors conduct research and publish their results. For many professors of computer science, the chance to do research is extremely important. And others supplement their incomes through consulting. The flexible schedule of the university gives them time for both research and consulting.

College instructors must hold graduate degrees. A Ph.D. in computer science is preferred, although because of the present demand, many instructors are employed with just their master's degree.

MEDICINE

The potential for computer applications in medicine is extraordinary: On the one hand, from billing to patient records to the day-to-day recordkeeping of a hospital, clinic, or private practice, automating medical records and billing has already improved health care productivity.

On the other hand, database software and computer networks provide physicians with instant access to information on poisons, rare diseases, and accident treatment. Information service providers let anyone access abstracts of the latest medical research. Even more intriguing possibilities exist in the development of systems that incorporate the knowledge of a doctor's lifetime medical practice. These systems not only assist experienced doctors and nurses, but they can be used by medical practitioners in rural or remote locations where doctors are not available.

Computers have even been used in the area of mental health, and PC products that let you act as your own therapist also exist. This computerized feedback technique has proved remarkably successful, as many people find it easier to express their troubles and anxieties to a computer than to a human therapist.

Bioengineering—engineering applied to develop sophisticated technology to test and treat health problems—also relies increasingly on computer technology. In the future, computer science and engineering, bioengineering, genetic engineering, and robotics will combine in ways that even the most imaginative science fiction writer cannot conceive of today.

INFORMATION SCIENCE

Information scientists use their knowledge of computers and information processing techniques to design large information storage and retrieval systems. These systems let users obtain specific information from computer storage easily, quickly, and reliably.

Information scientists develop methods to collect, organize, and classify information for computer storage and retrieval. They then construct, maintain, and update the system they have designed. Information scientists often specialize in particular fields, such as agriculture, medicine, education, or chemistry. This is because they must have some understanding of the information to be classified. Automated searches of stored information are done using key words or descriptors. Thus, the system must be designed and key words selected according to the logic of the field itself.

Information science is closely related to library science, for these large information systems are essentially vast electronic libraries. In fact, you can think of information scientists as the librarians of the future. Information scientists are employed wherever there are large quantities of information to be organized. Employers include commercial data banks and computerized information services, large corporations, and government agencies, including the Library of Congress.

OPERATIONS RESEARCH

Operations research (OR), also known as decision or management science, applies scientific principles to decision making. The OR specialist analyzes a problem, then uses the computer to mathematically or statistically model (or simulate) the effects of alternate decisions. OR is used to determine how best to design, operate, or manage systems to optimize the allocation of resources and people.

OR specialists work with man-machine interface problems, automation and robotics, land use and highway planning, financial planning and forecasting, medical decision making, meteorology, ecology, and in many other areas of modern life.

Whether their subject is a hospital, a company, a production line, or an electrical power grid, OR specialists view things as a system. When applied to manufacturing and automation, OR is a tool of industrial engineering. Although similar in many ways to (and often overlapping with) systems analysis, OR is distinguished by its heavy reliance on mathematics and statistics, modeling, and computer simulation.

By its very nature, operations research is an interdisciplinary field. OR analysts hold undergraduate degrees in many different disciplines. To become an OR specialist requires a strong quantitative background, including courses in probability and statistics, linear algebra, economics, and, of course, computer science. Some colleges offer undergraduate degrees in operations research or management science. Some programs in industrial engineering, systems analysis, or management emphasize OR methods. However, most work in operations research requires graduate study. Typically, a student with an undergraduate degree in math, computer science, management, or engineering will go on to specialized graduate study in OR.

CHAPTER 5

PREPARING FOR A CAREER IN COMPUTERS

The most common way to enter the software profession today is through completion of a four-year program in computer science or a related program such as business analysis or information management.

However, not all software designers have a computer science degree. Many colleges now offer majors in business and information management that combine a technical education with business skills. For many information systems professionals, it makes more sense to follow this path rather than pursue a strictly technical degree. And some major computer companies seek out students with liberal arts or other majors for entry-level positions in customer support and other areas. As the new employees learn more about the companies' products and technologies, some of them will move into software development, quality assurance, or marketing. Other companies consider students with two-year degrees for some entry-level jobs, because they do not have to offer as high a salary as they would to a graduate with a bachelor's degree. Nevertheless, many companies still require a four-year technical degree as a condition of hiring.

What is true for software developers also is true for information systems professionals. Advanced software development tools make it possible to produce software applications without writing computer code in a language like C or C++.

PREPARING FOR THE FUTURE

Your best bet to securing a well-paying job in software development and information systems is still to complete a four-year degree program in computer science or a related field. At the same time, keep the following in mind:

- Competition for good jobs with good companies is the rule.
- Technical skills alone are not sufficient.
- Creative thinking is an important element of solving software development problems.
- Technology changes rapidly.

Finally, in today's world, most people will change careers not once, but two or three times throughout their working life. Keep this in mind as you acquire the education and training you need to enjoy a career in software.

Top executives in information systems are occasionally selected for their talent at understanding business needs, their ability to think creatively about how computer resources can be applied to achieve business goals, and their leadership skills at motivating the people with whom they work.

LEARNING ON YOUR OWN

If you or your family owns a personal computer, you can increase your computer knowledge by writing your own programs using software tools available that will let you explore and learn on your own. Also, users' groups abound. Participation in these loosely organized groups of enthusiasts is a great way to develop your software skills, as well as to meet interesting, like-minded people of all ages and occupations.

You also can learn about computers and software by taking part in on-line forums, accessing information on the Internet, and reading books and periodicals.

HIGH SCHOOL

If you are still in high school, what can you do to begin to prepare for a career in computer science? We can offer you four points of advice:

1. Follow a solid college-preparatory course of studies with an emphasis on mathematics and English.
2. Learn as much as you can about computers and computing.
3. Develop good study habits.
4. Begin planning for college as early in your high school career as possible.

It is never too early to begin to plan for college. By the end of your junior year, you should be making concrete plans for your college education. If you have decided that computer science appeals to you, you will want to read the following sections in this book on selecting a college. Choose four or five colleges you think you might like to attend, and write for copies of their catalogs, admission requirements, and information on housing, financial aid, and other topics. Most schools require that students submit their results on the Scholastic Aptitude Test (SAT). These tests are offered at a limited number of locations several times each year, and you must arrange to take them in advance.

In addition to standardized tests of academic achievement and ability, many colleges and universities have other admission requirements. You may need to have taken a given number of credit hours in English, social studies, science, math, or foreign languages. Some schools also will ask you to write an essay explaining your reasons for seeking admission to their school. They may want you to visit their campus for an interview with a campus admissions officer or provide letters of recommendation.

If you plan to go to college, you should be enrolled in a college preparatory program in high school. Your course work should include solid training in mathematics, especially if you are interested in the theoretical or engineering aspects of computers and computer science. Physics also is recommended. Good communications skills will be crucial to your success in college and beyond. Take as many English courses as you can, especially those with a strong emphasis on writing. A course in public speaking or speech communication will further improve your confidence and self-expression, helping you to communicate effectively with others.

Needless to say, you should take every opportunity to learn as much as you can about computers and computing.

If your high school offers courses in programming, by all means take them. If your school has a computer club, you will certainly want to become a member.

Admission to the better colleges and universities requires good grades. A record of solid academic achievement will increase the likelihood of your acceptance by the college of your choice. Development of good study habits and a commitment to perform at the peak of your ability will encourage your academic success in high school. And good study habits and self-discipline will be essential in college. Writing and debugging programs, learning about computer science theory and practice—these things demand concentration, patience, attention to detail, and time. If you cannot discipline yourself to study intensely and to set aside significant amounts of study time and use that time effectively, you stand little chance of doing well in college. Each year, some college freshmen fail to make it to their sophomore year because they never developed good study habits while in high school.

TWO-YEAR JUNIOR AND COMMUNITY COLLEGES

Many two-year junior and community colleges offer associate degrees in computer-related studies. An associate degree may help you to obtain an entry-level job with some companies or small businesses. However most professional-level positions in computing require a four-year college degree. Certainly, you will enjoy better wages with a four-year degree.

If you decide to attend a two-year college and to transfer later to a four-year school, it is important to follow a general course of study that will satisfy the requirements of the college or university to which you wish to transfer. Be careful to take a wide range of general requirements. A narrow emphasis on computer or technical courses may jeopardize your admission to the college of your choice. Also, many colleges and universities will not accept all credits transferred from another school. This is especially true of requirements in your major field. You will cause yourself the fewest problems and potential disappointments if you discuss entrance requirements and transfer policies in advance with admissions officers from your chosen four-year school. You then will be able to plan your junior-college curriculum so that you meet those requirements.

FOUR-YEAR COLLEGES AND UNIVERSITIES
Selecting a College or University

In selecting a college or university, you should be guided by a number of considerations, including:

- the strength of the computer science program
- computing facilities
- the general reputation of the college or university
- location, cost, and availability of student loans and other financial aid
- the campus

Undergraduate Curriculum

The core of your undergraduate curriculum will consist of courses in computer science theory and applications. You can expect to be assigned many lab or homework problems that will require extensive time on the machines.

You will also enroll in required and elective courses in mathematics, natural sciences, the humanities, communication skills, and the social sciences. You will probably take at least a few courses in another engineering field or in business. Courses in business will be especially helpful if you plan to work in corporate IS or as a consultant.

Mathematics is clearly an important field of study for computer scientists. Mathematics will be especially important if you plan to work in scientific fields or in operations research. For others, courses in statistics are highly recommended.

Most colleges and universities have established science requirements for students in each major. The majority of engineering programs include four or five courses in general sciences. For the computer science student, physics is a clear choice. The fundamental laws of physics involved in electricity, electrostatics, electromagnetism, thermodynamics, mechanics, and even optics are central to understanding the principles of computer technology. In addition, you may want to consider courses in biology or biomedical sciences, especially if you are interested in the medical applications of computer science or in human factors and cognitive psychology. Linguistics, semantics, and formal logic also can be helpful in certain areas of computer science research and application. Physiology courses can be useful in human-factors study and in robotics and problems in human-machine information processing, as well as in neural network research.

The humanities include history, philosophy, literature, and the fine arts. Most colleges and universities require that students complete a number of humanities courses to ensure that their graduates are well-rounded, literate individuals. As a student in computer science, you may find courses in the humanities (and the social sciences) a refreshing change from your technical studies. Learning to appreciate art, literature, or music, and becoming informed about the history of human culture, will enrich your life in ways you will appreciate for years to come. Course work in liberal arts may well prove useful, as well as interesting, if you aspire to management. Recent studies of the college background of senior executives show a strong correlation between achievement in the business world and a college education that stressed the liberal arts.

Classes in technical writing, technical editing, and advanced composition (emphasizing practical rather than literary writing) will help you write functional specifications and market requirements documents, as well as help you document your code for those who maintain it.

In business applications, management, marketing and sales, and consulting, oral communications skills are essential. Courses in speech communication, including technical or professional speaking and group or organizational communication, will help you develop these skills.

The social sciences include anthropology, psychology, sociology, political science, and economics. Most colleges require some course work in these subjects. Psychology, especially cognitive psychology, will prove useful to students interested in artificial intelligence, pattern recognition, or human factors.

For students interested in information systems jobs, economics courses are important. The study of economics will help you understand the fundamental principles underlying modern business and financial transactions and decision making. Banking and financial services depend on today's information technology; there is a good chance you will work for such an organization. Political science will give you a better comprehension of the ways in which economic and political structures are affected by computer technology.

In selecting engineering courses, choose courses that will be of service to you in the context of your career goals. If you are interested in hardware, drivers, and utilities, course work in electronics, instrumentation, or control theory will supplement your work in electrical engineering. If you are interested in computer-aided manufacture and robotics, courses in advanced mechanics and industrial engineering are appropriate. A good advisor in your computer science department can help you to select these courses wisely. Course work in data and telecommunications is also very important.

For those interested in business applications, systems analysis, or information management, the study of accounting, finance, and management is essential. Other degree programs emphasizing a range of computer applications in business and industry include systems analysis, systems engineering, industrial engineering, management science, and operations research. Most of these programs place less emphasis on the theoretical and engineering aspects of computers and more emphasis on practical problems of providing automated systems to do the work of business and industry.

Financial Aid

Although publicly funded institutions are generally less expensive, tuitions have risen dramatically across the United States. Furthermore, changes in government funding continue to make it more difficult for students to finance their education. In addition to basic tuition and fees, you will need to pay for room, board, books, supplies, and incidental expenses. These costs mount up rapidly.

There is no doubt that obtaining a college education is worth this expense. A college degree is a ticket to higher-paying and more responsible jobs in many fields. A college education also gives you a rich foundation in cultural and historical knowledge that will enhance the quality of your life.

If you need help paying for college, types of financial aid include: 1. grants and loans based on a student's simple need; 2. grants and loans based on a student's (or a student's family's) ability to pay; 3. work-study programs; and 4. scholarships, grants, and awards made in recognition of a student's accomplishments or academic potential. Sources of financial aid include federal and state governments, foundations, civic groups, fraternal organizations, professional organizations, individual colleges and universities, and major corporations.

Many other sources of financial assistance are available, including state aid, college funds and scholarships, private scholarships, and employee tuition reimbursement programs.

Part-Time and Summer Employment

Many students help pay for the cost of their education by taking part-time jobs during academic terms or full- or part-time jobs during summers. One kind of work, though, should be pursued wholeheartedly. Any computer-related work experience you gain during school terms and summers will be useful to you. The sensible computer student will seek out jobs in the computer lab or at the help desk. Such experience will increase the meaningfulness and relevance of your course work. Moreover, employers seek out graduates with computer-related work experience in entry-level hiring. Computer professionals and employers are unanimous in stressing the benefits of this experience. Alternately, seek out opportunities to volunteer your services helping others to master aspects of computer and networking use. Many organizations will value this experience as much as on-the-job experience.

Intern or Cooperative Programs in Industry

Working in the computer industry during summers or as part of a cooperative education or internship program can give you valuable experience. You will gain a firsthand knowledge of the real-world work environment. And you will greatly expand your knowledge of computers and computing. Furthermore, many students who do well as interns or co-op workers receive offers of employment when they graduate.

GRADUATE STUDY

For many individuals, graduate school will be an attractive option. There are a number of reasons why you may wish to seek an advanced degree. Some positions in research and development require at least a master's degree and, in some cases, a Ph.D. Individuals aiming for management positions, especially in corporate IS, will find that an M.B.A. (Master of Business Administration), combined with an undergraduate computer science degree, will make them very attractive to employers. And a graduate degree in computer science, usually at the master's level, affords those with undergraduate degrees in other disciplines entry into the computer field. Finally, the Ph.D. is generally necessary to teach computer science at the college level.

The Master's Degree in Computer Science

The master's degree requires a minimum of thirty-two to thirty-six semester credit hours of study beyond the bachelor's degree. Some programs require completion of a thesis; others offer thesis and nonthesis options. You will, however, probably need to complete some kind of original research or programming project. You will certainly have to pass a comprehensive oral or written exam.

Two groups of people will benefit from taking a master's in computer science. First, if you wish to specialize in a certain area, such as computer architecture or software engineering, but are not ready or willing to commit yourself to a lengthy doctoral program, graduate study at the master's level may be your answer. If you are considering working toward a Ph.D., but want to test your aptitude and interest in graduate-level study, a master's program gives you this opportunity. After a year, you can leave academic study and take a job in industry or you can continue toward your doctorate.

A second group finds that the master's degree gives necessary proof of qualifications for employment in the computer field. These are people whose undergraduate degree is in another discipline, often in the liberal arts or social sciences. For these individuals, a good way to change the direction of their career is to obtain a master's in computer science, information management, or a related field.

If you are entering the computer field from another discipline, most computer science departments will ask you to successfully complete a number of undergraduate courses before admitting you to their master's program. This is necessary to give you the basic knowledge upon which your graduate courses will build. And it demonstrates to the department your ability to undertake more advanced study.

Before making a career change, it is best to enroll in one or two computer courses. If you do well and, more importantly, if you enjoy computing, then make plans to study for your master's if you believe it will enhance your job opportunities.

Because the demand for skilled software professionals is great, if you can demonstrate a high level of technical knowledge and ability to produce results, a master's degree is not necessary. Employers look at what you can do to help their business succeed, not at how many degrees you have collected.

The Ph.D. in Computer Science

Doctoral study allows you to do original research in computer science and qualifies you to teach in colleges and universities and to perform advanced research in industrial settings or research institutions, if that is where your interests lie.

CERTIFICATION

Many professions, such as law, medicine, or accounting, have certification procedures to ensure that their members are competent. There are no industrywide certification standards for computer professionals. In fact, plumbers are subject to stricter licensing requirements than are computer professionals. However, the Institute for Certification of Computer Professionals (2350 East Devon, Suite 115, Des Plaines, IL 60018, www.iccp.org) addresses this problem. The ICCP is a nonprofit organization established for the purpose of testing and certifying the knowledge and skills of computer professionals. Its constituent societies include most of the major professional organizations in the computer and data processing field. Certificates are awarded on the basis of tests administered twice annually at selected sites throughout the United States and Canada and overseas.

Certification is more meaningful outside than within the computer industry. If you plan to work in corporate information systems, certification can be a valuable credential. Few, if any, programmers working as software developers for hardware and software vendors have certification of any sort.

COMPANY-SPONSORED EDUCATION AND TRAINING

Your education in software and information technology does not end when you receive your college degree. In many ways, it is just beginning.

For the first six to eight months you are on the job, you will be learning about company equipment, software, and procedures. This training may be formal or informal. How well you do during this initial period can affect your future success, as many employers see this as a probationary period.

Because of the rapid rate of technological change in the computer field, most larger companies offer many opportunities for the continuing education of their employees. Many sponsor both internal and external educational programs.

Internal training programs range from career improvement courses offered through the human resources department to seminars on specific technical issues. These courses may be supervised and staffed by the company educational services division or by outside consultants.

Many employers encourage their workers to go outside the company to further their education. Many sponsor employee enrollment in M.B.A. programs to prepare technically knowledgeable people to move into management. An especially valuable benefit to you as an employee will be your company's tuition reimbursement program.

Some companies offer classes at their facilities taught by faculty from nearby colleges and universities. Companies that invest in employee education consider their money well spent. Their investment pays off in better educated, more up-to-date employees who are informed about advances in the computer field and better able to perform their jobs. A technologically obsolete employee is of little worth in a field as dynamic as computer science.

KEEPING UP WITH NEW DEVELOPMENTS

Because software and information change so rapidly in the information systems field, it is particularly important that you take steps to stay current with new developments throughout your career. There are many ways of doing this:

Read. Many magazines are available that cover most changes in hardware, software, and information systems management methods. Increasingly, these periodicals are available on-line.

Join a professional organization. Professional associations are another fine source of keeping up to date in an enjoyable way. These associations usually have monthly meetings in major cities with speakers amd seminars on topics of current interest to the members. They also have annual conferences of two or three days with experts in their specialties. Most such groups have technical journals, which are included with membership.

Attend seminars. Many organizations conduct one- to five-day seminars in major cities on the latest technical subjects. These often can be helpful in becoming educated on a particular subject. They usually cost several hundred dollars, and most who attend have the seminars paid for by their employers.

Go to sales presentations. Vendors of hardware and software often put on demonstrations or classes as part of their marketing programs, and these presentations are a good source of information about the products covered. Check the business section of your local newspaper for information.

Go to trade shows. Trade shows and exhibitions are conducted in major cities in which many computer software, hardware, and services vendors have booths and exhibits displaying their products and services with marketing representatives to explain what their companies have to offer.

Go on-line. Subscribe to one or more of the on-line information services or Internet providers. A wealth of up-to-date information about computer hardware, software, and related topics is available on vendor Web pages on the Internet, on CompuServe, and on America Online.

CHAPTER 6

FINDING A JOB IN COMPUTERS

Here are some common methods to help you find a job in computer-related careers.

RESEARCHING EMPLOYERS

There are a number of ways to find out about potential employers and bring your qualifications to their attention. Job openings are advertised in newspapers, trade journals, and on the Internet. Some general employment guides are published each year, and you can write directly to a company inquiring about openings. You can use personal contacts to get a foot in the door, or you may find your first job through campus recruiting efforts on the part of large employers.

Large employers of computer specialists sometimes obtain a list of graduating students from computer science departments or schools of engineering. You may receive a letter from such an employer (or from the United States military). You can always contact a prospective employer directly, submitting a letter of application, together with your resume, which outlines your qualifications and interests. If it is convenient, you also might visit a company and talk with someone about the kinds of work done at that facility. Many companies will gladly talk to interested individuals about their work. Such informal contact sometimes can lead to later employment.

Your computer science professors may be able to assist you to find a suitable position. Many professors maintain contacts with industry, and some work in industry as consultants.

In addition, your participation in student chapters of professional organizations may help you in your search for employment. These organizations frequently sponsor guest speakers from business, industry, and the academic world.

Another way to find out about potential employers is to join a computer users' group in your community. PC user groups are now found in almost every part of the United States. Through users' groups, you can meet other computer enthusiasts and exchange information and software.

ON-CAMPUS RECRUITMENT

Many large companies in the computer industry send recruiters to colleges and universities with large or outstanding programs in computer science. The campus recruiter will visit with qualified students interested in working for his or her company. These interviews are arranged through the school's career guidance and placement office, and you may have to sign up for interviews several weeks before the actual interview date.

On-campus interviews are basically screening interviews. Few, if any, job offers will be made. More likely, successful candidates will be invited, at company expense, to visit company facilities. During this "plant trip," you will spend a day talking to a range of company personnel and will learn firsthand what it would be like to work for that organization.

RESPONDING TO ADS

Many software development and information systems positions are advertised in trade publications and in the classified section of major metropolitan newspapers. The Sunday editions of the *New York Times,* the *Boston Globe,* and the *San Jose Mercury News* have numerous listings, including many jobs that lie outside their geographic areas. National employers will advertise in these widely read papers. Most of the positions will call for experienced personnel, but not all companies that regularly hire recent graduates advertise entry-level positions.

If you do find a position for which you are qualified, you must respond promptly. The earlier your response is received, the better chance you will have to be actively considered for the job. Include in your ad response letter those measurable results that relate to what the ad says the employer wants. Try to have an accomplishment statement for each qualification the ad calls for.

USING PROFESSIONAL RECRUITERS

The use of professional recruitment services is common in the software and IS job market. Technical recruiters—often referred to as "headhunters"—are contracted by potential employers to hunt down the right candidates. Recruiters can make sure your resume gets to the individual who makes the hiring decision.

Many engineering and computer science employment agencies are located in major centers of the computer industry. When you go through such an agency, you'll work with a specific headhunter who will seek to match your skills with available openings in a variety of companies. The best headhunters develop ongoing relationships with several companies and hiring managers. When a manager needs a new employee, he or she often turns first to a headhunter who has provided good employees in the past.

Executive search firms are another source of possible openings. They obtain a fee for making a match between candidate and employer. Search firms usually handle higher-level positions, up to top-officer levels. They often have an exclusive contract to fill a position on a fixed fee or contingency basis, and they usually seek out people who are not necessarily looking for a job and try to lure them into considering their clients.

TECHNICAL JOB FAIRS

Technical job fairs bring together in one place many different companies seeking to hire qualified people trained in computer science and other technical and engineering disciplines. At job fairs, employers set up information displays and company representatives talk informally with interested individuals about their company and its work. Because of the demand in recent years for computer-savvy personnel, these job fairs have become a very popular way for employers and potential employees to find out about each other.

ON-LINE JOB RESOURCES

When surfing the Internet, you might be pleasantly surprised at the amount of job-search information to be found on-line. One valuable reference book to guide you in your Internet job search is the *Guide to Internet Job Searching,* by Margaret Riley Dikel and Frances Roehm, co-published by the Public Library Association and VGM Career Books.

Your Internet account can help you find a job, provide you with vital information about prospective employers, and give you a fast and convenient way to communicate with potential employers. As with all business activities on the Internet, it pays to be careful in using the Internet to look for a job.

Many on-line services usually have thousands of job listings from all parts of the United States as well as overseas. Many of the jobs are senior level or contract positions. You can use key-word searches to narrow your job search, and job listings frequently include salary information.

Finally, many companies maintain their own Web pages. If you are preparing for an interview, thinking about accepting a job, or just curious about a company, visit its website.

RESUMES

Resumes come in many styles, including:

Chronological. The chronological resume lists your education and work experience, starting with your most recent position and working back in time. For each job, you include your title, dates of employment, employer's name, and a description of your responsibilities and duties and accomplishments. The most common form of resume, the chronological resume is also the one many college students will use when seeking their first job, especially if they have work experience.

Functional. The functional resume organizes your experience according to your major areas of knowledge or accomplishments, rather than in simple chronological order.

Targeted. The targeted resume is a hybrid form that includes information found in both the chronological and the functional resume—information about your education, work experience, and skills.

When preparing your resume, decide if you want it to be scannable or not. For scannable resumes, use nouns rather than verbs and no bullets or underscores. For nonscannable resumes, use action verbs. Bullets and underscores also may be used on resumes that will not be scanned.

Regardless of the style of resume you use, you will want to cover the following information:

- your name, address, and phone number
- education
- work experience
- computer languages and equipment experience
- professional affiliations and activities
- special skills

You also need to line up individuals willing to provide recommendations for you well in advance of your job search. Professors and previous employers will be your best sources of professional references. Personal or character references can be provided by anyone who has known you well and can speak for your integrity and other character traits.

Always ask an individual if he or she feels able to recommend you. The more your references know about your work, your ambitions, and the job you are applying for, the more effective their recommendations will be.

PREPARING FOR A JOB INTERVIEW

It is extremely important to prepare for a job interview by finding out as much as possible about the company you will be visiting. A trip to the library can help. Or you can look up the company on-line. Newspaper and magazine articles also give the most recent information about how and what a company is doing and are good for finding out about technical developments as well as company problems.

What kinds of questions can you expect an interviewer to ask? Most interviewers will want to know about your academic background: which courses you enjoyed, which you did not like, and how your education prepares you for the opportunities their organization offers. They will ask you about your extracurricular activities, interests, and work experience. You may be asked to identify your strengths and accomplishments—and your weaknesses. Interviewers look for candidates with clear career goals. The more you know about the kind of work you want to do in the computer field, the better you will be able to respond to questions about your career direction. And many interviewers will want to know where, based on what you know about their operations, you see yourself most effectively working. Again, note that the best-prepared job candidate has done his or her homework on the company.

Some other general guidelines to help you interview successfully include:

- Be punctual.
- Dress professionally.
- Be personable.
- Ask questions.

Be sure to obtain the interviewer's name, title, and company address. Within a day or two of your interview, write a short follow-up letter, thanking the interviewer for taking time to talk to you about the company. You might point out a feature of working with that company that particularly interests you, and you should express your continuing interest in employment.

Most interviewers will tell you when you can expect to hear from them. If they do not, be sure to ask them for a date. You can do this gracefully by pointing out that you are interviewing with other companies and would like to know when you can expect their decision to be made.

In general, approach the interview and your overall search for employment with these thoughts in mind:

- Employers hire *people,* not degrees.
- Employers prefer people who set clear career objectives.
- Assuming your education and skills are appropriate, the most important aspect of an interview or site visit is the chance for both you and your prospective employer to see how you "fit" with one another. This concept of "fit" or suitable match is crucial to your future success at a given company.

SOME PRACTICAL SUGGESTIONS

Experienced job hunters know that the search for employment can itself become a nearly full-time job. Finding a job takes research skills, organization, and persistence, even in the computer field where so many opportunities exist. Plan to devote a considerable amount of time and energy to your job search. If you are still in school, you may want to plan your last semester so that you have enough time to look for employment without sacrificing your academic standing.

Some very practical suggestions include:

- Buy yourself a personal organizer. Write down appointments, interviews, and dates you can expect to hear from employers. Also record all telephone conversations and the dates you send out letters and resumes.
- Keep copies of all correspondence with employers. You may need to refer to this correspondence.
- Be persistent and follow through on all leads. If you send out a job letter and do not receive a response within two to three weeks, write or telephone the employer to inquire about your status. If an interviewer says that you will hear from them in three weeks and you do not, make a phone call. Your papers may have been lost in the shuffle.
- Do not take rejection personally. Your qualifications and your style will not suit the hiring needs (or styles) of all employers. This does not make you any less qualified.

EVALUATING EMPLOYMENT OFFERS

When you receive an offer of employment, there are a number of factors you should consider before accepting the job, especially if you are trying to choose among more than one offer. Some things to think about include:

Benefits. It may seem strange to be thinking about retirement when you have not yet started your first job. But retirement, life, health, and dental insurance; disability coverage; and investment plans are no less a part of your total salary than is your basic wage. Companies also vary in their vacation, holiday, personal day, and sick day allocations.

Other specific benefits to consider are 401K and employee stock purchase plans, profit sharing, and employee incentive options. A 401K plan allows you to save a percentage of your income before taxes, thus reducing your overall taxable income. The 401K plan is meant to be a savings plan for retirement. However, you can borrow against it or take out money in certain cases: for instance, to buy a house or in the case of a major illness in your family. Your 401K plan can be transferred when you change employers. Many employers match a certain portion of your 401K contribution. This can prove to be a very attractive savings plan.

Employee stock purchase plans allow you to purchase shares of your company's stock at a discount, usually at the lower of the beginning and ending price during a designated period. Stock plans encourage employees to invest in their own future. If the company does well, the employee, as a shareholder, also benefits.

Some companies in the computer industry also have profit-sharing plans, letting all workers share in a percentage of profits. Employee incentive options reward valuable employees by giving them an opportunity to purchase blocks of stock at a considerable discount. As an entry-level employee, you should not expect to be recruited with promises of options. As you progress in your career, however, it will be something to ask about, especially when considering employment with a small or start-up company.

Finally, many companies offer tuition-reimbursement programs to their employees. Education is expensive, so tuition reimbursement can be a very attractive benefit. Many people in the computer industry pursue their master's degree in a part-time program or simply take courses at company expense to keep up-to-date while working full-time.

You may find it difficult to read through the description of employee benefits, which may be written in opaque and legalistic language. Try to make a list of benefits provided by the employer and calculate their worth. In comparing two employers, one offering a higher salary, the other better benefits, subtract the value of those benefits from the more attractive salary to see what you really will be making.

Geographical location. The cost of living in different parts of the country varies dramatically. A high salary for Dallas or Atlanta may not go very far in San Francisco or Boston. You need to decide how important living in a particular city, state, or region is to you. You also may need to accommodate your geographical preferences to the realities of the job market. Are you more concerned with what you do or where you do it?

Opportunities for advancement. Will a position allow you to grow and develop professionally? What opportunities will you have to move upward and outward in the organization? Will working for this employer help you to achieve your career goals? What is the employer's policy regarding promotions?

Employment security. A young, expanding company may offer opportunities for rapid advancement. At the same time, it may be financially less stable. Do you seek the security of an established company, or are you attracted by the advantages and risks of a more volatile organization?

Company culture. Some companies are conservative in appearance, attitude, and procedures. Some foster competitive, fast-paced, intense working conditions; others are more measured, relaxed, or stratified. Try to match your own characteristics to the style of an organization. Select the employer with whom you will feel most comfortable.

INTANGIBLE JOB SATISFACTIONS

When evaluating possible career directions or prospective employers, remember to consider the intangible satisfactions as well as the salaries and benefits that you can anticipate. These intangible rewards vary, of course, because of the many different types of jobs within the software industry. Also, different people will find satisfaction in different aspects of a given job.

Some of the kinds of satisfaction that professionals in the field of software have found include:

- a good feeling at being part of a field that is in the forefront of innovation and change in business, government, and our individual daily lives
- the enjoyment of seeing specific beneficial results from your individual work effort, such as an easier system, lower costs, better quality, or customer satisfaction
- gratification at being part of a team, working with people you like
- contentment with a programming or research position where you find and resolve problems

Finding a Job in Computers 85

- satisfaction gained from being a part of a project with a beginning and end, of successfully bringing a product to market or seeing your software deployed throughout your company
- the feeling of being respected in playing an advisory or supportive role and for sometimes being considered an expert

CHAPTER 7

SHAPING YOUR CAREER

In this chapter we will look at a number of factors that will be important to you as you shape your career as a computer professional. These include geographical distribution, industry trends, entry-level salaries, your possible career path, and the possible opportunities for advancement. Finally, we will touch briefly on some of the major technical and business directions that will be a factor in employment over the next several years.

GEOGRAPHICAL DISTRIBUTION

A large number of computer positions are located in major cities: New York, Boston, Los Angeles, San Francisco, and Dallas-Ft. Worth have large concentrations of computer professionals employed in a variety of industries. The federal government is a major employer of computer professionals in every department, and many computer companies maintain sales and marketing offices in the Washington, D.C. area that focus on selling to the federal government.

However, because of the volatility of the industry, you need not live in a major metropolitan area to enjoy a successful career in computers. Every region of the United States offers job opportunities. In information processing and business applications, opportunities exist in banking, insurance, financial services, manufacturing, health care, education, and government. In fact, the major growth segment for sales of computer hardware and software in recent years has been to small businesses. Furthermore, more and more people are working from home offices. Small businesses, home office workers, and consumers all will require varying levels of computer services.

Telecommuting has had a major influence on expanding the limits of geography for people working with computers. Advances in telecommunications and decreases in the cost of communications mean that more and more software developers can work from home. The bottom line is that as a software professional, you enjoy more freedom of choice in where you work than do professionals in many other industries.

DEMAND

The demand for software professionals is expected to continue to grow much faster than average through the year 2005, according to the Bureau of Labor Statistics. The rate of growth, however, will be somewhat slower than it was during the 1970s and 1980s, as the computer industry has matured to become one of the largest American industries.

Contracting is one trend that may be especially appealing to people for whom job flexibility and continual new challenges is important. Increasingly, computer vendors and other businesses hire programmers on a contract basis for a single project. These projects may last from a few months to a year or more. Rather than having to lay off employees at the end of the project, employers are turning to contract workers to meet their programming needs.

Contractors are usually paid on an hourly basis. They often make more per hour than full-time employees. However, they generally do not receive the additional benefits—vacation, sick days, health and other insurance, investment and retirement accounts—that full-time employees enjoy.

Few people are hired as contractors for development work right out of school. Contractors are specialists and must come prepared with the skills needed for the project in question. With a few years' experience, though, many people enjoy the freedom that contracting affords, which allows them to spend more time with their children, to travel, or simply to move on to a new project.

TRENDS THAT MAY AFFECT DEMAND

Although the overall demand for software professionals is expected to expand rapidly over the next several years, demand for some technical skills will inevitably diminish. The proliferation of the networked personal computer, combined with the growing use of smaller, more powerful computers as servers, has meant than many businesses are reducing their reliance on the traditional large mainframe computer. Although mainframe computers will persist, the role these machines play in a company's information systems architecture is already changing. Primary business applications that once were run on these "host" machines are now distributed on smaller computers in the trend to downsize computer operations. At the same time, the vast amount of data that today's information-intensive business operations require means that the mainframe computer plays a key role in storing vital company information. Therefore, while demand for traditional mainframe programmers will decline, demand for skills in mainframe computers will persist, although at a lower level than in previous years. The changing role of the mainframe computer is only one example of the ways in which technological and business changes affect demand for programmers and systems analysts.

The lesson to be learned from this is that the demand for specific technical skills changes rapidly in the computer systems field. In order to stay competitive, you need to stay on top of market trends and keep your own skills in line with those trends.

In addition to changing trends in technology, two other factors may affect the demand for software professionals over the next few years: outsourcing and globalization. Outsourcing is the subcontracting of systems and data processing design, implementation, and maintenance to outside service organizations. Companies outsource some or all of their information systems work because they expect that it will cost less and free management to focus more on its own products and services. This trend is reducing the number of information systems specialists needed within individual companies. On the other hand, it increases employment opportunities with service organizations, consulting organizations, and systems integrators.

A second trend that will affect employment in the coming years is the globalization of business. Although many computer vendors are expanding their overseas market share, the globalization of business means many jobs that once might have been performed in the United States can now be done more economically in other countries.

It is still too early to say what effect globalization will have on salary and overall demand for software professionals in the United States. Nevertheless, it is important to keep in mind that, in the words of Edith Holleman, counsel to the U.S. House of Representatives' Science, Space and Technology Committee, high-tech jobs "are not reserved for you in the First World." All the more reason to maintain and refresh your technical skills throughout your career.

SALARY STATISTICS

The website www.dice.com recently showed the top ten contract jobs and the top ten IT full-time positions that pay the highest salaries (see figures).

Also, take a look at the following list of median earnings for a variety of careers in the computer industry. Please keep in mind that earnings may vary according to the region

Top Ten Positions–Contract Jobs

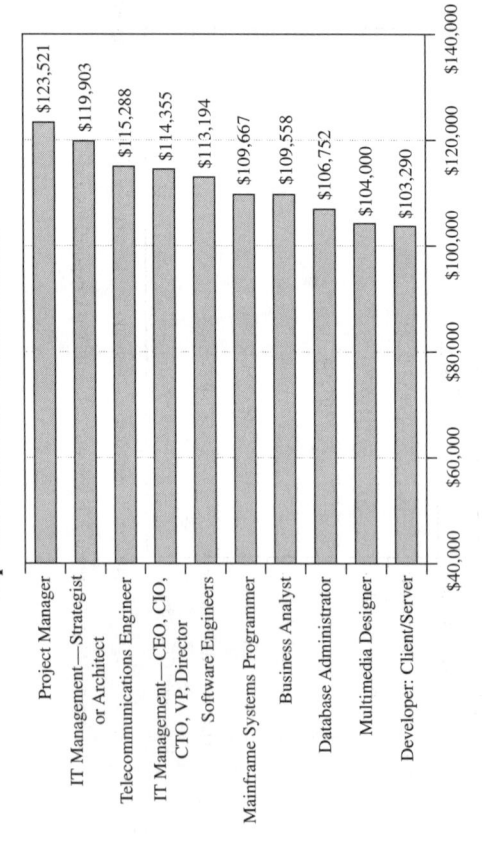

Position	Salary
Project Manager	$123,521
IT Management—Strategist or Architect	$119,903
Telecommunications Engineer	$115,288
IT Management—CEO, CIO, CTO, VP, Director	$114,355
Software Engineers	$113,194
Mainframe Systems Programmer	$109,667
Business Analyst	$109,558
Database Administrator	$106,752
Multimedia Designer	$104,000
Developer: Client/Server	$103,290

Source: http://marketing.dice.com/rateresults/top-ten-positions.asp

Top Ten IT Positions–Full-Time Jobs

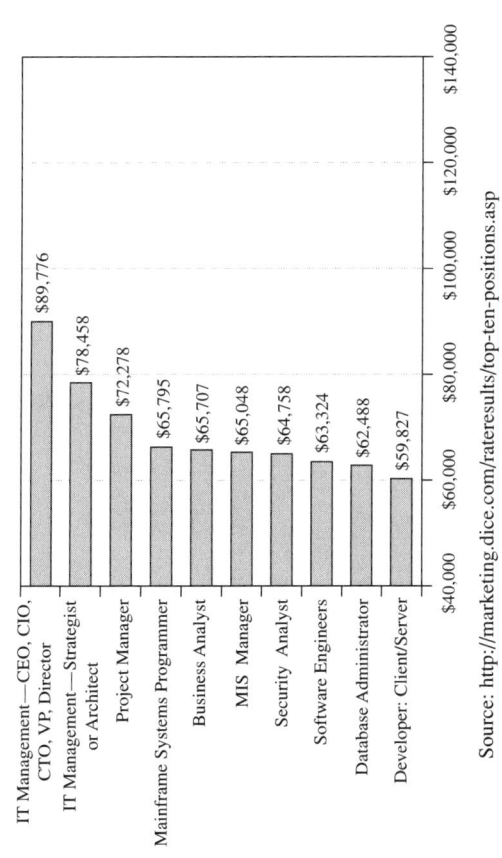

Position	Salary
IT Management—CEO, CIO, CTO, VP, Director	$89,776
IT Management—Strategist or Architect	$78,458
Project Manager	$72,278
Mainframe Systems Programmer	$65,795
Business Analyst	$65,707
MIS Manager	$65,048
Security Analyst	$64,758
Software Engineers	$63,324
Database Administrator	$62,488
Developer: Client/Server	$59,827

Source: http://marketing.dice.com/rateresults/top-ten-positions.asp

of the United States, cost of living, demand, and other variables. The *Occupational Outlook Handbook,* published by VGM Career Books, offers up-to-date employment outlooks and salary statistics for hundreds of careers.

Median Earnings by Title

Job Title	Median Low	Median	Median High
Management Level			
CIO/ Vice President	$132,800	$168,900	$194,500
IS Director	104,900	115,000	146,500
Manager, Systems Analysis & Programming	87,600	100,200	120,000
Manager, Systems Programming/ Technical Support	86,200	96,800	116,700
Network Manager LAN/WAN	78,300	90,900	113,200
Systems Analyst/Programmer/ Project Leader	73,300	82,500	95,500
Database Administration Manager	89,700	100,200	121,600
Manager Telecommunications	86,300	102,800	118,900
Internet Architect	81,200	91,100	105,800
Data Center Manager	63,000	75,100	100,000
PC Work Station Manager	55,800	67,500	85,100
Professional Staff			
Senior Software Engineer	71,000	83,900	99,200
Software Engineer	56,300	69,000	81,300

Job Title	Median Low	Median	Median High
Senior Database Analyst/Administrator	70,000	86,200	104,700
Object-Oriented/GUI Developer	63,100	77,900	93,500
Web Developer	76,500	86,700	99,200
Network Administrator LAN/WAN	64,200	74,300	84,900
Senior Systems Analyst Programmer	66,100	72,000	80,600
Systems Analyst Programmer	58,900	64,700	77,900
Senior Systems Administrator/Unix	64,700	71,800	83,300
Senior Client Server Programmer/Analyst	68,300	76,100	88,000
Client Server Programmer/Analyst	61,900	69,100	80,000
Senior Mid/MF Programmer Analyst	60,300	71,200	79,100
Mid/MF Programmer Analyst	48,800	61,700	68,500
Telecommunications Specialist	44,400	63,000	78,500
PC Applications Specialist	44,400	51,000	59,900
Quality Assurance Analyst	57,100	70,200	84,000
Security Specialist	73,100	86,000	110,600

ADVANCING ON THE JOB

Almost without exception, your first position upon graduation will be as a programmer, junior programmer, or quality assurance engineer. From this point, your advancement will depend on your abilities and interests, your initiative, and the career goals you set for yourself.

Two paths of advancement are open to you: a technical path and a path leading into management. Companies have now made dual-paths of advancement available to their employees. New job titles and responsibilities have been created in the technical domain. An employee still can advance into management. But successive levels of technical promotions have been created, in recognition of the fact that many computer professionals will be happiest and most productive if technical avenues of promotion exist.

Large- and mid-size computer hardware and software vendors offer many opportunities to pursue a technical career path. Large vendors offer additional opportunities for the technical person to move laterally into marketing, sales, or customer support.

Within vendor organizations, you can move both vertically and laterally. This means that you might move from a technical position into a position in marketing or technical support, or from one design project to another. Such diversified experience within a single company is a good preparation for advancement into the higher levels of management.

Within end-user organizations, you can move vertically as well as laterally. Until recently, MIS departments were structured like a pyramid, with programmers on the bottom and MIS directors at the top. Three trends have changed this: 1. the increased use of networked desktop PCs and client-server applications; 2. corporate restructuring that makes individual business units within a company accountable for more decision-making (reducing several layers of management, including IS management); and 3. a move to relocate some information systems staff in individual business units. The growing importance of information technology to large organizations has created a new structure under the authority of the CIO or Chief Information Officer.

Typical Career Paths

Following is a list of some typical career paths of individuals who have spent a number of years in computer-related positions. This will give you a small idea of what you can expect in real-life situations and how long it will take you to progress. At times in the past, individuals stayed with a single company throughout their career. Today, however, this is less common. More typically, an individual will work for many employers.

- programmer to entrepreneur—fifteen years
- programmer to chief database architect—eight years
- salesman to vice president of data processing—fifteen years
- programmer to consulting firm owner—twelve years
- engineer to placement branch manager—twenty-five years

- correspondence clerk to chief information officer—twenty-five years
- programmer to director of information systems—twenty-three years
- mail clerk to senior vice president of corporate planning—forty years

Note About Equality of Opportunity. Individuals of any sex, race, creed, or ethnic origin can do well in computer science. Because computer science requires mental, not physical, skills, it can be a good choice for those with physical disabilities. People with limited vision, hearing, and mobility have found successful careers in the computer field.

TECHNOLOGY AND MARKET TRENDS

In the coming years, the following technological advances will be among the factors that drive the computer industry:

- the continued increase in computing power
- migration of corporate mission-critical applications from mainframe or minicomputers over to desktop systems and development of client-server applications
- easier-to-use software based on the use of intelligent systems
- hardware and software targeted for specific markets

- networking and telecommunications
- the growth of the Internet and on-line services
- multimedia
- the growth in home computing

CHAPTER 8

COMPUTER-AIDED DESIGN (CAD) AND COMPUTER-AIDED MANUFACTURING (CAM)

FIVE MAJOR TECHNOLOGIES

Five major technologies are involved in programmable automation. They are:

Computer-aided design (CAD). Simple forms of CAD are used as an electronic drawing board, often by drafters and design engineers. CAD also can help a designer or engineer make changes in an existing product. In more complex and sophisticated installations, CAD is combined with computer-aided engineering (CAE) to help engineers analyze and improve designs, through modeling and simulation, before products are actually built.

Numerically controlled (NC) tools. NC machine tools are devices that follow programmed instructions to cut or form a piece of metal. The instructions tell the machine the desired dimensions and the steps for the process. The term CNC refers to computer-numerically controlled machine tools.

Flexible manufacturing systems (FMS). A computer-integrated group of clusters of multiple NC machines or workstations. They are linked together with work-transfer devices for the complete automatic processing of different product parts, or for the assembly of parts into differing units.

Industrial robots. An industrial robot is basically a manipulator that can be programmed to move objects.

Many countries and users have accepted the definition of the Robotic Industries Association (RIA), for what a robot is: "a reprogrammable, multifunctional manipulator designed to move materials, parts, tools or other specialized devices, through variable programmed motions for the performance of a variety of tasks."

Robot technology ranges from simple pick-and-place robots to intelligent robots that can decide actions by means of their sensing function and their recognizing function.

In today's industrial world, robots with grippers perform tasks in such fields as die casting, loading presses, forging and heat treating, and plastic molding. They load and unload other machines. A different kind of robot—one that can handle a tool instead of grippers, or uses its grippers to grasp a special tool—is used in applications like paint spraying, spot or arc welding, and in grinding, drilling, and riveting in machining.

Computer-integrated manufacturing (CIM). In computer-integrated manufacturing, programmable automated tools are used for design, manufacturing, and management in an integrated system, with maximum coordination and communication between them. Computer-aided manufacturing (CAM) is just one part of an integrated system; it is with CIM that the most dramatic gains in productivity and cost-savings are being made.

THE CAD/CAM/CAE INDUSTRY

Four major sectors make up the computer-aided design, computer-aided manufacturing, and computer-aided engineering industry. They are:

Mechanical CAD/CAM/CAE—This involves tools used to design, analyze, document, and manufacture discrete parts, components, and assemblies.

Electronic design automation (EDA)—This involves tools used to automate the design process of a variety of electronic products. EDA has several segments: electronic computer-aided engineering, integrated circuit layout, and a printed circuit board multichip module.

Geographic information systems (GIS)—With these systems users capture, edit, display, and analyze geographically referenced data. GIS/mapping software, which often uses CAD technology for basic drawing, combines graphics, computer images, and database management software to map or analyze geographic and demographic information. A GIS program usually contains a series of digitized maps based on a database of data and measurements, information about relationships among the data, and a database of alphanumeric (letters and numbers) data that describe features of map areas, lines, or points.

Architectural, construction, and engineering—This is computer-aided software used by architects, contractors, and plant and civil engineers to aid in designing and managing buildings and industrial plants. ACE software will also have significant growth because the U.S. government is demanding that small commercial developers provide it with electronic design data for government-contracted building projects.

HOW CAD WORKS

Although no one can accurately predict the future of this industry, CAD is an essential part of a new technology—Rapid Prototyping & Manufacturing—that's helping industries increase competitiveness because it saves costs and time. RP&M is a vehicle for turning basic research and design work into finished products faster, with higher quality, and at lower cost.

The key to CAD is computer graphics—the use of the computer to display graphic images. The images are based on mathematical coordinates, which are just like points drawn on a graph for a geometry class. This descriptive information exists in the computer as digital electronic data. The computer makes it possible to store, retrieve, transmit, and process these data quickly and accurately, and the monitor shows the data as drawings.

At the heart of every CAD system is a computer, which works with the data the CAD operator supplies. There are several methods for giving data to the computer. One technique uses a mouse—a small, handheld device that's moved either mechanically or optically across an array of lines on a small pad. As the mouse "runs" across the lines, it counts them, sending information to the computer about how fast it is moving and how many times it has moved. The computer uses this information to move an indicator (typically a cursor, crosshair, or indicator circle) around the screen.

Of course the CAD operator can type on a keyboard, sending information about the coordinates and typing in commands, just as he or she would type a letter. It's also possible to send information from another computer to the computer the CAD operator is working on, connecting the computers directly.

Another way of transferring CAD information between computers is by using a modem—a device that lets computer equipment talk to other equipment through phone lines or computer cables. Such information is "read" by the CAD operator's computer just as if the operator had entered it on the computer, using a mouse, stylus/digitizing pad, or other input device.

The computer gives back the information it's received, using various forms of output devices to let the CAD operator see how the computer is manipulating the data. Usually the CAD operator sits in front of a monitor.

Another common output device is a graphics plotter. A simple form of graphics plotter may be a dot matrix printer, operating in the "graphics mode," drawing points on a piece of paper, one point at a time. A more complex plotter might use a technical pen that follows the computer's commands and draws a picture on a piece of paper. Sometimes the paper is stationary, and the pen moves in both directions. At other times, depending on the particular plotter, the paper may move in one direction, and the pen may move in another.

WHAT THE CAD OPERATOR DOES

A typical CAD operator sits in front of the terminal and keyboard. He or she may be working on CAD with a single stand-alone personal computer, or at a computer that's part of a local area network (LAN). The mouse, digitizing tablet, stylus, or input device is just inches away, so the operator can reach it easily.

Sometimes a rough paper design already exists for a product. If so, the CAD operator can use the system's digitizing capabilities—the ability to "read" or trace the geometric shape from the paper drawing. Or an operator can use a separate scanner. The computer transforms the information into a series of geometric coordinates, or points, and puts it into its memory. Then the CAD operator can manipulate the drawing on the screen.

Or, perhaps the shape the operator wants is similar to something that's already been CAD-designed. Many companies maintain CAD libraries of files. The operator can tell the computer to retrieve the drawing—or desired details—

from the CAD library or from its memory. It's similar to picking out a book from library shelves or calling up a text file containing a previously keyed-in letter. Once the existing design or detail has been "read" into the computer's memory, the CAD operator can edit it, just as an administrative assistant can make changes in an old letter. When the desired changes in the designs are completed, the edited design can be stored again for later recall.

Typically, a CAD system has a library of designs and commands that have been stored. Much as word processing software has commands already stored that let the keyboarder delete, re-form paragraphs, or move blocks of type from one location to another in a manuscript, a CAD system contains commands that let the operator erase, redraw, or move portions around the screen. Of course, there also are commands that let the operator perform many more functions.

CAD's real productivity, many users believe, is that by automating the routine work of replicating objects, CAD frees up time. "Designers can spend more time actually designing," says one point-of-purchase designer. "Or we can develop designs to a certain point, and give them to other CAD operators to finish the details."

2-D AND 3-D CAD

The image the operator draws on the computer screen is, of course, two-dimensional (having height and width, but not depth). In the CAD world, however, there is a difference between 2-D and 3-D. Unlike a paper drawing, a photograph, or a painting, the computer-screen image can

108 *Opportunities in Computer Careers*

be manipulated as if it were a real 3-D object. For example, an operator can instruct the CAD system to rotate the object, so he or she then sees another face of the object.

CAD technology and systems are changing rapidly. The first generation of CAD and 2-D CAD might be described as computerized drafting systems. They reduced traditional dependency on drawings and related paperwork.

HOW CAD AND CAM FIT TOGETHER

Ideally, computer-aided design (CAD) and computer-aided manufacturing (CAM) are parts of a broader concept: computer-integrated manufacturing (CIM).

Many CAD systems can—and do—go beyond computer-aided drafting. CAD lets an operator or designer work out the physical dimensions of the product and the steps necessary to produce it on the computer. Disks containing the information can be used by computer-aided manufacturing equipment.

Some CAD systems let the operator "see" the machining process on the screen and help to guide the operator through various steps in planning the machine process. The system may be able to produce a tape that can be fed into a machine tool controller and used to guide the machine tool path. Under conventional manufacturing processes, a manufacturing engineer would interpret design drawings and establish plans for the machine to make the required part.

Sophisticated CAD systems are important components of computer-aided engineering (CAE). Of course, the

CAD system makes it easier to perform drafting and design changes. Engineers also can use CAD systems to visualize how a product will work, or to get an estimate of its performance.

CHAPTER 9

WORKING IN CAD

At the heart of CAD technology is the computer—the data-crunching machine that manipulates figures and digitized points to allow drawing and drafting, refining, and even finite element analysis. To those with vision, CAD is far more than just a computer program that lets users draft and design. Being able to use CAD isn't enough to guarantee you a job, however.

THE CAD FIELD

If you want to enter the CAD field, you must have:

- ability to read and understand manuals
- teamwork skills—both on, and off, the job
- ability and willingness to follow instructions, without being a hot shot
- good CAD drawing skills—plus some mechanical knowledge

It's certainly realistic to expect that you may be able to find part-time work, even as a high school student, if your

CAD technical skills are good, if you market yourself aggressively, and if—once on the job—you continue to learn. But if you *really* want to succeed in tomorrow's workplace, you almost certainly will need additional skills. Increasingly, experts are recommending a series of specific "I can do" competencies as a necessary ingredient for moving up.

The typical user of a CAD system might be a design engineer, often spending five to six hours a day on a computer, much of it on a $2\frac{1}{2}$ D system. A CAD system manager works with a whole range of people: designers, engineers, structural analysts like mechanical engineers, or structural engineers who do manufacturing and tooling. The CAD system becomes the hub for all of them. Computer-aided manufacturing bridges the traditional gap between design and production people.

Groups of a dozen or so CAD stations have a system administrator, who's responsible for the electronic files, making backups, transferring data fields, and making sure the system is up and running.

CAD IN INDUSTRIAL ENGINEERING

In industrial engineering, computers are used to improve manufacturing efficiency. Computer applications include numerical control, computer-aided design and manufacture (CAD/CAM), and robotics.

More recently, computer-aided design and manufacturing (CAD/CAM) have come into wide use. CAD relies on very high-power, high-resolution graphics workstations and software that allow engineers to draw a part or product design on the video monitor. This eliminates time-consuming drafting and redrafting of various stages of the design. When the design is perfected, it can be printed and serves as the basis for manufacturing specifications. CAD applications have been widely adopted in the automotive and electronics industries, as well as by architects and other designers.

Computer-aided manufacture (CAM) uses a hierarchy of computers to control many facets of the production process. The most highly publicized element of CAD/CAM is undoubtedly robotics. Robots, for all the mystique the word evokes, are really just extremely flexible computer-controlled machines. A numerically controlled machine can be programmed to different specifications, but it can still only perform one task. A robot, on the other hand, can be programmed to manipulate a range of tools or to perform a number of different tasks.

Industrial engineering and robotics offer many attractive career opportunities. People will be needed to design the manufacturing tasks that robots will perform, to design the workplace in which they operate, and to program the machines. If you are interested in engineering applications of computer technology and have some mechanical inclinations, you might consider industrial engineering as a career option. The Society of Manufacturing Engineers (www.sme.org) has a strong student program. This group can give you further information about industrial engineering, CAD/CAM, and robotics. See also Chapter 11 on "Working in Robotics."

CAD IN POINT-OF-PURCHASE

The point-of-purchase (P-O-P) industry, which includes everything that's used in stores to display, promote, and advertise specific products, is a $15 billion industry in the

United States, and probably $30 billion worldwide. As most buying decisions are made in the store, high-quality displays for in-store merchandising are important. Increasingly, the behind-the-scenes technology that designs and produces those displays is depending on CAD—and, to a lesser degree, on CAM. That's because CAD has special advantages.

- CAD lets P-O-P designers be innovative, because they can model ideas on screen as well as on paper. Experimenting with new ideas is easy.
- CAD lets P-O-P designers turn designs around more quickly, because CAD lets them make changes virtually on-the-spot to suit clients.
- CAD offers the ability to replicate—to make twenty-four identical boxes on screen, or to take a space of a certain size and subdivide it, filling each portion with an identical model of a client's product. The designer doesn't have to hand-draw each element in the display.
- CAD designs can be archived. If a design used formerly can be pulled from a library of data files and modified, the designer doesn't have to start again from scratch. CAD is a cost-effective use of a designer's time.

With a CAD data storage bank of files, a company can use the same stored image over and over. Moreover, the data can be shared—not only with design firms, but also with ad agencies, who use the files for pickup photography or product imagery.

Another use of CAD is called *planogramming*. Store owners, especially those whose stores are part of a nationwide chain, can draw a grid electronically on screen and "place" products on the grid the way they will appear on the shelves in the store. The technology gives the retailer and manufacturers a way to test the optimum placement of product.

CHAPTER 10

WORKING IN CAM

Computer-aided manufacturing varies from industry to industry, and among companies within industries. Different manufacturers are at different stages in their use of automation technologies. Consequently, it is not possible to list all available CAM jobs. Instead, this chapter includes brief descriptions of the technology and some thoughts on how those in the industry view the future. A number of trade magazines cover developments in CAM and factory automation. Keeping up with industry news and trends is one of the best ways to monitor the industry.

WHAT CAM IS

Before you can look at the effects of CAM on employment opportunities in today's manufacturing environment, you need to think about what is meant by *computer-aided* manufacturing. The U.S. Congress's Office of Technology Assessment says computer-aided manufacturing includes robots, computerized machine tools, and flexible manufacturing systems. Also included are numerically controlled (NC) and computer numerically controlled (CNC) machine tools. All are considered "programmable automation" tools for design, manufacturing, and management. To the extent that a company integrates the system, we say that the company is using *computer-integrated manufacturing* (CIM, pronounced "sim.")

Just as computers have changed since they were originally introduced, so have these machines changed as "new" CNC technology pays off in productivity. For instance, thirty-two-bit processors offer today's CNCs more substantial computing power than earlier machines. Another development in manufacturing teams CNC mills and machining centers with laser digitizers—devices that use laser light to scan structures and turn their measurements into digital signals. Sometimes the data the laser "reads" are blended, through sophisticated software, and eventually exported to a CAD/CAM system. The CAD/CAM system then develops a surface model for machining a tool.

WORKCELL CONTROL SOFTWARE

CAM technology isn't limited to giant manufacturing companies and huge automated factories. It can work very well in much smaller environments. A firm that spots opportunities and develops niche products to fit a perceived need can be successful.

Workcell control software is a subset of the CAM market. This software makes an electronic connection between working instruments and a larger data system. One of the vendors who offers workcell control software is Hudson Control Group, Inc., a company that specializes in connecting work instruments (including small robots) to larger data systems.

PROCESS CONTROL JOB OPPORTUNITIES

There are two sets of technical positions: engineers who are not programming specialists, but who know how to design machinery and electrical systems; and computer programmers, who are able to do sophisticated programming. Minimum qualifications for both: a four-year degree—with good grades—from a "good" college with a national reputation. Good communication skills, for both sales and technical staff, are also important.

EXPECTATIONS OF GRADUATES ENTERING THE FIELD

Companies that interview engineers who are graduating expect them to have had training in CAD/CAM. And since computers are becoming so powerful, some employers will emphasize "virtual reality"—a technology that can be described as intensive CAD/CAM and computer applications of 3-D design work.

You also should be prepared to relocate, if necessary, and think nationally when you're job-hunting.

Many people think that most CAD/CAM opportunities for entry-level graduates will come in aerospace and automotive industries. But that's not necessarily true in today's economic climate. Those wanting to work in CAD/CAM and manufacturing should look at packaging companies—companies in which products are processed, packaged, and shipped.

Additional opportunities may exist in systems integration companies—smaller, engineering service companies that contract with larger firms to solve those companies' automation problems.

CHAPTER 11

WORKING IN ROBOTICS

Industrial robots have received a great deal of attention in recent years . . . far more than they did in 1961, when the first industrial robot was used commercially. The vision of an automated factory in which robots and machines work together to turn out products at high speeds is not that far from reality.

Although a career in robotics sounds exciting and challenging, how realistic is it to assume substantial opportunity exists? Robotic Industries Association (RIA), the association of suppliers and users of robots and robotic components, compiles industry figures on use and shipments. Economic conditions are expected to improve in the North American market because companies that have been putting off large capital equipment expenditures will no longer be able to delay these investments. In addition, the growing pressure on U.S. companies to improve productivity and product quality requires manufacturing executives in virtually every industry to examine possible solutions.

GROWTH IN THE ROBOTICS INDUSTRY

The U.S. robotics industry has a very long way to go before robots are sold in the kind of numbers that they should be in North America.

It's difficult to compare statistics because countries define "robot" differently. RIA defines an *industrial robot* as "a reprogrammable multi-functional manipulator designed to move material, parts, tools or specialized devices, through variable programmed motions for the performance of a variety of tasks." RIA uses that definition to track sales and use. The Japanese, however, define *robot* in broader terms.

WHY ROBOTS?

Many large industrial corporations have begun to move into flexible automation. They've invested in technology and have retrained personnel in order to stay competitive in the global marketplace. Many of them have reduced labor costs substantially—some, to as low as 10 percent of the total cost of production.

The Move Toward Automation

Several factors may be part of the reason robotics has not (as yet) lived up to early hopes, for the technology. In the United States, many small- to medium-size businesses have found it difficult to raise the money needed to modernize and automate. Regulations such as those from OSHA and EPA, the high cost of U.S. labor (and benefits, including health care), and accounting practices that govern how capital investment is reported make it difficult for them to maintain the profit margin to which they've been accustomed.

And industrial robots are expensive. Automation always involves a capital investment that must be amortized through cost savings on each unit produced. Because investing in a robot may not yield a return for a number of years, a small business may be reluctant to spend the money required to buy it, or it may be unable to convince a lender to finance the improvement.

Another reason small companies have been reluctant to invest is because equipment they have in place may not be being used to its fullest potential.

SERVICE ROBOTS

According to the National Service Robot Association, wherever people want their skills augmented, such as in relieving humans from hazardous jobs, performing security functions, or helping the developmentally disabled, robots are beginning to appear on the scene.

Growing numbers of robots are used in education, health care, security, training, space, and military operations. Within Robotic Industries Association, a specialty association called the National Service Robot Association (NSRA) represents builders, developers, and users concerned with this application of technology.

Why Use Service Robots?

Companies that use service robots see them as a cost-effective way of accomplishing tasks. For instance, the health care industry is looking for ways to decrease costs, while still keeping—or even improving—the quality of patient care. Labor costs, especially when benefit costs are factored in, are high. Consequently, hospitals, clinics, and nursing homes are looking at all internal operations, seeking areas where productivity can be increased. Among other issues, they are studying ways to improve "fetch and carry" tasks. It is inefficient, health care administrators believe, to use highly skilled (and highly paid) hospital personnel for these tasks.

No one knows exactly what these trends may mean to your future in CAD/CAM, and especially in the robotics side of the industry. Technologies such as machine vision and simulation (and its "cousin," a new software development called *virtual reality*) all hold promise. You will want to monitor developments closely to see what implications they have for the career choices you will be making.

CHAPTER 12

EDUCATION AND TRAINING LEAD TO JOBS IN CAD/CAM

JOB-HUNTING TIPS

Finding your first job in CAD/CAM may not be as difficult as you'd imagined, particularly if you are proficient in CAD. Here are some tips that apply specifically to CAD/CAM or related technologies; others are fairly general. If you are graduating from a community college or technical institute, you should be working closely with your school placement office to help you arrange job interviews. If you are graduating with an engineering or engineering technology degree, your college or university can often schedule interviews for you with company recruiters who visit the campus. Often, your placement office will critique your resume. Counselors may even videotape you in a mock job interview, analyzing your strengths and weaknesses so you can improve how you come across to potential employers.

There are several strategies you can use to improve your chances, even before you are actively job-hunting for a full-time position. One is to work part-time in CAD while you are going to school or receiving technical training.

Major papers in large cities often specify CAD experience as a prerequisite for applicants. Even though you may not yet have worked full-time in CAD, if you can show a prospective employer that you have hands-on experience with a particular CAD package, as well as a desire to succeed in the field, you may be able to negotiate a part-time position as a fill-in, a temporary extra hired to help with a work overload, or a vacation replacement.

Another strategy is to become a co-op student, alternating semesters on campus with time spent on the job. Engineering graduates who've done this have an advantage over those who haven't, say many recruiters.

Get involved early in your college years. Join trade associations, especially those with student chapters. Go to the trade shows, symposiums, and conferences—not only in CAD/CAM, but in related fields, like robotics, machine vision, and other areas of manufacturing technology. You'll find calendars of upcoming events in the industry trade magazines.

Trade associations have chapters in major cities. Guests can almost always attend a single meeting for a low fee. Regular monthly meetings feature speakers, and often include plant tours. Attending meetings (and becoming active in a chapter) are good ways of getting contacts that may later lead to employment.

All the trade associations listed in the appendix of this book publish papers, journals, and books. Buying and reading those in your particular field of interest will help you keep current on technology, as well as on the nontraditional issues facing today's CAD/CAM personnel.

COMPETENCIES AND SKILLS TO SUCCEED

Below are five workplace competencies and a three-part foundation of skills and personal qualities that effective workers need for solid job performance in this field:

- Resources—They know how to allocate time, money, materials, space, and staff.
- Interpersonal skills—They can work on teams, teach others, serve customers, lead, negotiate, and work well with people from culturally or economically diverse backgrounds.
- Information—They can acquire and evaluate data, organize and maintain files, interpret and communicate, and use computers to process information.
- Systems—They understand social, organizational, and technological systems. They can monitor and correct performance, and they can design or improve systems.
- Technology—They can select equipment and tools, apply technology to specific tasks, and maintain and troubleshoot equipment.

Here are the foundation skills competent workers in the high-performance workplace need:

- Basic skills—They can read, write, do arithmetic and mathematics, speak, and listen.
- Thinking skills—They have the ability to learn, to reason, to think creatively, to make decisions, and to solve problems.
- Personal qualities—They possess individual responsibility, self-esteem and self-management, sociability, and integrity.

This combination of workplace competencies and foundation skills is not taught in many schools or required for most diplomas. Nevertheless, your chances of succeeding in CAD/CAM or a related career are better if you can perform these tasks.

If you do possess these competencies, have a degree or advanced course work, and have experience in an architectural firm or engineering-related jobs, you can get hired in CAD/CAM.

TRENDS

As you begin to plan your career in CAD/CAM, especially if you are emphasizing manufacturing technology, there are several trends you'll have to monitor.

- Offshore sourcing—in which companies put together parts and components overseas, where production costs are lower—has become a significant factor in today's manufacturing.
- Another trend you'll need to watch is the move toward concurrent engineering as manufacturers rethink the traditional design process.
- Synchronous manufacturing is a third trend you should watch. The term refers to a time-based competitive strategy that focuses on moving material through a factory more quickly.
- Simulation—computer software that makes it easier for engineers to answer "what if" questions—is also becoming widely used by companies with high-value manufacturing programs. Simulation software can be combined with CAD systems to help companies meet rapidly changing production requirements.

Education and Training Lead to Jobs in CAD/CAM 129

Global economy. Concurrent engineering. Synchronous manufacturing. Simulation. They're big terms and big concepts. It is important *for you* to monitor them if you want a job in CAD or CAM because today's manufacturing methods are changing quickly. Since businesses are rethinking traditional methods and processes, trends like those listed above have implications for the number of jobs available, and you are going to have to take a much more active role in planning your career than might have been the case several years ago. You can't wait for a counselor or professor to predict what is going to happen. You'll have to read the business periodicals and the trade magazines. You'll need to decide for yourself how best to modify your training so you'll be able to compete effectively in the job market.

Specifically, the trend toward the global economy and offshore sourcing means that someday you may work overseas, using CAD, CAM, or both technologies. Your coworkers may be locally hired and trained, or you may work in the United States at a company owned by a foreign corporation. Either way, the employee who has fluency in a second language, who is aware of cultural diversity, and who understands how to work effectively in a multicultural team—and who also has sophisticated CAD and CAM skills—has a far greater chance to move up than a worker who's proficient in CAD/CAM, but who doesn't see the big picture.

The push for concurrent engineering means you may be using CAD and simulation tools to design in safety and efficiency up-front, before a product is ever made.

Synchronous manufacturing and simulation also are related to potential CAD-related jobs. Since "work-in-process inventory" (a term used in cost accounting for the cost of uncompleted goods still on the production line) doesn't produce money for a manufacturer, any method (including CAD) that speeds up a factory through-put helps the company's bottom line.

RESEARCHING EDUCATIONAL OPPORTUNITIES
CAD and CAM in Architecture and Design

If you'd like to study CAD with the idea of a career as an architect or designer, there are several ways you can find schools that emphasize such courses.

You can ask your school or public librarian to do a computer search using a database called "Peterson's." The librarian can then do a subject search for you, using "computer-aided design," "computer-aided drafting," "CAD," and other related terms to get a list of schools.

Another way to locate information is to consult the *College Blue Book,* published every two years, and almost certainly on your library's reference shelves. Look for the volume titled "Degrees Offered by College and Subject." Under "computer-aided design and drafting technology," you'll find schools that teach it. Your librarian can help you get addresses for the schools. Then write to them directly.

One of the most effective ways to get school, training, and career information is to consult the *Encyclopedia of Associations,* published annually by Gale Publishing, Detroit. The volumes are indexed in a unique way; read directions on how to look things up, or ask your librarian to explain the procedure. Check listings of national associations for architects and designers. Usually associations will have career information, as well as material on schools and colleges that offer programs. Write for information.

CAD and CAM in Manufacturing

One of the most effective ways for you to research information on this option is to buy the *Directory of Manufacturing Education*. It's affordably priced and available from the Society of Manufacturing Engineers. Included in the comprehensive directory is information on more than 550 colleges, universities, and technical institutes that have degree programs in manufacturing and related areas—including courses in CAD and CAM. Listings include degrees and course offerings, cooperative education and evening programs, and complete names, addresses, and phone numbers of persons to contact.

ABET-accredited manufacturing programs are indexed. So are programs at colleges with associate degree programs, bachelor's degree programs, and master's- and Ph.D.-level degree programs.

Finally, one of the most important things to remember about CAD and CAM is that each is just one part of technology used in automation. Both need to be looked at as part of a larger system, rather than as stand-alone technologies.

APPRENTICESHIPS

Apprenticeship is another way in which occupational training takes place. Today, apprenticeship is a businesslike system designed to provide workers entering industry with comprehensive training that exposes them to practice and theory. Generally this training is a combination of structured on-the-job "how to" and related theoretical information.

In the United States, the government defines an apprenticeable occupation as one that is usually learned in a practical way through a structured, systematic program of supervised on-the-job training. The occupation involves manual, mechanical, or technical skills and knowledge that require a minimum of two thousand hours of on-the-job work experience.

Federal and state apprenticeship agencies recognize more than eight hundred occupations as apprenticeable. Although CAD/CAM isn't one of them, such related occupations as architectural drafter, electronics technician, and engineering and scientific programmer are listed. Write to the nearest agency for information.

CHAPTER 13

INTERNATIONAL JOB OPPORTUNITIES

Many experts talk about the global market for products and services. Certainly, major companies, especially those in manufacturing, have already shifted production facilities overseas to take advantage of lower labor costs. Many companies are multinational—part of conglomerates controlled by investors from outside the United States. In addition, U.S.-based companies are entering into production agreements with factories in other countries. In short, high technology such as software, Web design, CAD/CAM, and robotics is by no means limited to one or two countries.

Today, technology is moving quickly, and the rate at which it's changing is faster than ever. In addition, political and economic developments have transformed traditional alliances. Consequently, your chances of finding a computer-related job in countries outside the United States are going to depend not only on your technical competency, but also on factors very much beyond your control, including the global economy, legislation, and international trade agreements such as the North American Free Trade Agreement.

For example, slow economic growth, coupled with an extremely competitive marketplace, have cut potential jobs in Europe. The unification of Germany and the consolidation of the European Community (EC) have already begun to impact on manufacturing there—in particular, steel, auto, machine tooling, and other heavy industry. Yet jobs in factory automation—the CAM side of CAD/CAM—may be a necessary part of Europe's catchup strategy.

SOFTWARE

Possibly as a consequence, manufacturing software—systems that handle CAD/CAM, manufacturing execution, and factory data collection—is on the upswing.

Tying systems together in networks—electronic data information exchange—also may be an area in which jobs will expand. *Fortune* magazine predicts that "corporations will be linked into increasingly coherent networks that connect all varieties of computers—from big iron to laptops to the pocket devices of tomorrow. The servers—a term for the computers that hold the information, much as a library has collections of books—will act as central repositories of data, holding anything from corporate files to videos and voice-mail messages."

CAD/CAM and related technologies are a small part of that industry. But for you, they may be your career—in Singapore, in Taiwan, in Brazil, as well as in Canada, Australia, and the UK. There are tremendous opportunities worldwide in CAD/CAM and other computer-related industries. The only limit is your imagination!

APPENDIX

ASSOCIATIONS

For every career opportunity and interest, there is a corresponding professional organization that you should consider for membership. We will describe some of the larger ones in detail and provide addresses for the smaller organizations so that you may contact them directly for further information. In addition, the Internet is a vast source of information for professional societies, associations, and organizations that can be tapped with the simplicity of entering a keyword. There are also websites you may explore regarding accreditation and schools that offer the courses that you will need in your exploration. Job descriptions, mission statements, affiliations, salary surveys, educational opportunities, national and international chapters, conferences, and publications are among the many resources you can find on the Web. These also furnish an almost unlimited number of links to help you find information on companies and job requirements that you will need in your job search, as well as in your continuing education and networking.

Here are some organizations and resources that may help you:

Council for Higher Education Accreditation
One DuPont Circle NW, Suite 510
Washington, D.C. 20036

The Council for Higher Education Accreditation (CHEA) is a nonprofit organization established in 1996 that is a national policy center on accreditation for higher education, including colleges and universities, regional associations, national accrediting institutions for special missions, and higher education associations headquartered in Washington, D.C.

As such, CHEA serves as a coordinator of processes that improve accreditation, gathers and disseminates such information, encourages communication between educational institutions and accrediting agencies, and maintains quality and diversity through accreditation.

> Computer Sciences Accreditation Commission
> 111 Market Place, Suite 1050
> Baltimore, MD 21202

The Computer Sciences Accreditation Commission (CSAC) administers the accreditation process for computer science programs as the only commission of the Computer Sciences Accreditation Board (CSAB). CSAC is negotiating an agreement with the Accreditation Board for Engineering and Technology, Inc. (ABET) that will lead to integration of both organizations. It will include postsecondary baccalaureate programs to prepare students for professions in computer science. CSAB/CSAC is recognized by the Council for Higher Education Accreditation (CHEA).

> Accreditation Board for Engineering and
>   Technology, Inc.
> 111 Market Place, Suite 1050
> Baltimore, MD 21202

The Accreditation Board for Engineering and Technology, Inc. (ABET), when merged with CSAB, will recognize CSAB as one of their participating societies and CSAC will become a fourth commission, the Computing Accreditation Commission (CAC).

> Institute of Electrical and Electronics Engineers, Inc.
> History Center
> Rutgers-The State University
> 39 Union Street
> New Brunswick, NJ 08901

The Institute of Electrical and Electronics Engineers (IEEE) computer society has more than 100,000 members and is the self-proclaimed "world's leading organization of computer professionals." The society holds conferences, publishes journals, and sponsors student chapters and technical committees. The society has service center offices in Belgium and Japan, with nearly one-third of its members living and working outside the United States.

> The American Society for Information Science and Technology
> 1320 Fenwick Lane, Suite 510
> Silver Spring, MD 20910

American Society for Information Science and Technology (ASIST), whose slogan is "Leading the search for new techniques and technology to access information since 1937," sponsors conferences, publishes periodicals and books, and provides networking possibilities with other members.

Contact any one of these associations for further information on a career working with computers.

AAAS Hispanic Outreach Initiative
Directorate for Education and Human Resources
1333 H Street NW
Washington, D.C. 20005

American Association of University Women
1111 Sixteenth Street NW
Washington, D.C. 20036

American Indian Science and Engineering Society
1630 Thirtieth Street, Suite 301
Boulder, CO 80301

American Statistical Association
1429 Duke Street
Alexandria, VA 22314

Association for Computing Machinery
1515 Broadway
New York, NY 10036

Association of Medical Directors of Information
    Systems
61 Jordan Road
Keene, NH 03431

Automated Imaging Association
Robotics Industries Association
P.O. Box 3724
Ann Arbor, MI 48106

Computing Sciences Accreditation Board, Inc.
184 North Street
Stamford, CT 06901

IEEE Computer Society
1730 Massachusetts Avenue NW
Washington, D.C. 20036

Independent Computer Consultants Association
11131 South Towne Square, Suite F
St. Louis, MO 63123

Institute for Certification of Computing Professionals
2350 East Devon Avenue, Suite 115
Des Plaines, IL 60018

Institute of Industrial Engineers
25 Technology Park/Atlanta
Norcross, GA 30092

International Service Robot Association
P.O. Box 3724
Ann Arbor, MI 48106

Junior Engineering Technical Society
1420 King Street, Suite 405
Alexandria, VA 22314

Mexican-American Society of Engineers
P.O. Box 3520
California State University
Fullerton, CA 92634

National Action Council for Minorities in Engineering, Inc.
3 West Thirty-fifth Street
New York, NY 10001

National Council of La Raza
111 Nineteenth Street NW, Suite 1000
Washington, D.C. 20030

National Network for Minority Women in Science
AAAS Directorate for Education and Human Resource Programs
1333 H Street NW
Washington, D.C. 20005

National Society of Black Engineers
1454 Duke Street
Alexandria, VA 22314

National Society of Professional Engineers
1420 King Street
Alexandria, VA 22314

Professional and Technical Consultants Association
1060 North Fourth Street
San Jose, CA 95112

Robotics Industries Association
P.O. Box 3724
Ann Arbor, MI 48106

Robotics International of the Society of Manufacturing Engineers
P.O. Box 930
Dearborn, MI 18121

Society of Hispanic Professional Engineers
5400 East Olympic Boulevard, Suite 210
Los Angeles, CA 90022

Society for Technical Communication
901 North Stuart Street, Suite 904
Arlington, VA 22203

Society of Women Engineers
230 East Ohio Street, Suite 400
Chicago, IL 60611

Sun Educational Services
UBRM12-175
500 Eldorado Boulevard
Broomfield, CO 80021

U.S. Robotics
935 National Parkway
Schaumburg, IL 60173